FOBA /
Buildings

FOBA /
Buildings

Essays /

Katsu Umebayashi
Thomas Daniell

Michael Webb
Peter Allison
Kazuhiro Kojima

Princeton Architectural Press /
New York

Published by
Princeton Architectural Press
37 East Seventh Street
New York, New York 10003

For a free catalog of books, call 1.800.722.6657.
Visit our web site at www.papress.com

Editing: Linda Lee
Design: Jan Haux

Special thanks to: Nettie Aljian, Dorothy Ball, Nicola
Bednarek, Janet Behning, Megan Carey, Penny (Yuen Pik)
Chu, Russell Fernandez, Clare Jacobson, John King,
Mark Lamster, Nancy Eklund Later, Katharine Myers,
Lauren Nelson, Molly Rouzie, Jane Sheinman,
Scott Tennent, Jennifer Thompson, Paul Wagner, Joseph
Weston, and Deb Wood of Princeton Architectural Press
—Kevin C. Lippert, publisher

Library of Congress Cataloging-in-Publication Data

FOBA (Firm)-
    FOBA : buildings / essays by Katsu Umebayashi ... [et al.].
      p.   cm.
    Includes bibliographical references and index.
    ISBN 1-56898-527-4 (pbk : alk. paper)
    1. FOBA (Firm) 2. Umebayashi, Katsu, 1963-
3. Architecture—Japan—20th century. I. Umebayashi,
1963–II. FOBA (Firm) III. Title.

NA1559.F63A4 2005
720'.92'2—dc22
                                    2004029097

Table of Contents /

Acknowledgments /

Working on this book in parallel to our daily architectural tasks was a heavy burden at times, but there were also enjoyable moments when the mists would clear, and the ideas would flow.

These ten projects cover a period of ten years, and each was a response to the demands of a particular client. Although there is no reason why they should have a single, unifying concept, after reviewing and refining the material, I feel that the essence of this architecture lies somewhere in the interval between *action* and *object*. This may have always been my subconscious conceptual structure, which leads me to think that my work is somehow inherently Japanese.

I am deeply thankful to Akihiko Endo and the rest of the team in the office for their tireless efforts during my incessant demands to produce more material, and to my friend and colleague Tom Daniell for his painstaking work in assembling and editing it all. Even more so, I must thank all the clients who provided the opportunities to create these buildings; words are insufficient to express my gratitude.

Finally, for all their unstinting support throughout, I dedicate this book to my family, and above all to my wife, Satoko.

My thanks to you all!

Katsu Umebayashi

Nesting: Beyond Objects to the Bodily Experience of Space /

Katsu Umebayashi

Although the Japan in which I live can no longer be described as an economic super-power, the rest of the world may view the majority of the population here as enviably wealthy. Yet many of us here feel that the spaces of our daily lives are somehow impoverished. Why should that be so? It seems that the origin of this poverty lies partly in our architecture. With the motivation of simply trying to address this issue, I have devoted the last decade to designing small buildings.

Of course, phrasing it in that way makes it seem as though focusing on small buildings was a deliberate choice. In fact, it is because most of the design opportunities available to young Japanese architects are within the vast quantities of tiny, fully detached houses that are constantly being built all across the country. Yet despite the

familiarity and banality of these structures, I consider them to be intimately related to a variety of social problems, such as juvenile delinquency and social alienation. Small buildings possess the latent power to jolt our conventional conceptions about architecture.

Japan's chronic shortage of buildable terrain has resulted in a deeply entrenched "myth of land"—the illusion that real estate is an eternal asset. In the period following the Second World War, the Japanese public became such devoted disciples of American-style democracy that possessing one's own plot of land became a funda-mental aspect of the government's social policies.

Looking at the built results, it is clear that the desire of the average person for their own private house is so widespread that it has become even more prevalent than among our American role models. From farm village to metropolis, the entire nation has been swamped with endless arrays of fully detached houses. The impact of these small buildings cannot be ignored. The cumulative effect of their multiplication has been to shatter our sense of authentic place. The natural beauty of Japan is now just a poignant memory, blanketed by scenes of capitalist development. At a conceptual level, this is a result of our perception of wealth having been reduced to nothing more than the ownership of things. From the period of Japan's intense economic growth during the 1960s until the collapse of the so-called "bubble economy" in the early 1990s, the clearest indicator of personal economic success was to ostentatiously fill your home with consumer goods. We are only now coming to realize that we have been progressively obscuring the true wealth of our cultural history and natural environment. The apparent wealth of conspicuous consumption only disguises our actual poverty.

Can we invent methods that allow us to escape this systematic impoverishment? It has become a pervasive phenomenon that extends beyond the field of architecture,

afflicting every aspect of our lives. Although we may be in control of the processes that produce this phenomenon, our techniques are ineffectual in any situation other than the currently existing one—much like the way the theories and methods of Newtonian physics, Marxist economics, or Darwinian biology are only valid within circumscribed domains. Although the impact of this impoverishment is becoming increasingly clear, it remains insufficiently exposed and theorized.

Our sense of place is relentlessly eroded by the onslaught of information, by communication technologies, and by the volatility of contemporary society. In the field of architecture, we have abandoned our sensitivity to the specificity of place in favor of the neutral freedom promised by Miesian "universal space." Our former harmoniously integrated sense of place has been regimented and fragmented by modernist rationality; the notion of place no longer refers to a permanent location but to an arbitrary and changeable address. With our sense of place now partitioned to the point where it may be seen as an endless array of objects, these deterritorialized objects contain the potential to be reassembled into unprecedented configurations, resulting in new types of place. The creation of modernist universal space relies on a clear distinction between place and object, but in the real world their respective identities have become ambiguous—place is just another commodity to be owned or exchanged. Universal space is therefore now something that can only be produced in a test tube, not in the real world.

How should we build in a world of such total relativity, where places have become objects? Taking a more positive view of this situation, if everything is now relative, we may make design choices with absolute freedom. By treating all phenomena—time, place, history—as equivalent, they may be juxtaposed, superimposed, and blended at will.

Transcending modernist rationality, this new type of place may be assembled at any arbitrary location and is predicated on our ability to freely select materials from

the environment, like a bird assembling a nest. Such a nonhierarchical nest of found objects is a phenomenological mirror that reflects its surroundings. Making a nest is a process of accumulating objects, producing ambiguous boundaries that never result in completely isolated spaces. Here, then, is a new way for architecture to attain a sense of wealth.

FOBA: It's Not What It Looks Like /

Thomas Daniell

In examining Japanese architectural production of the last couple of decades, at least three distinct ways of responding to the urban context can be identified:

> To retreat—withdrawing behind blank walls in silence and solitude, open
>> only to the sky
> To reflect—mimicking the fragmentation and noise of the surrounding city
> To merge—dissolving into the kaleidoscopic blur of traffic, neon, and rain

However sensitive or critical—whether Tadao Ando's introversion, Shin Takamatsu's aggression, or Toyo Ito's "vanishing act"—each approach is ultimately an avoidance,

never an engagement. Context is treated as a generic external condition, not a specific arrangement of objects and spaces. Whatever the accompanying rhetoric, architecture maintains its autonomy, isolated from and indifferent to its neighbors—and given the "chaos" of the Japanese city, perhaps that was an appropriate stance to take.

But that was then. If the disparate work of the emerging generation of Japanese architects has a unifying theme, it is contextual relationships. This is not a rejection of the methods of their predecessors—who are also their former teachers and employers —but an inevitable process of extension and adaptation.

Drawing on the legacy of architect-professors such as Kazunari Sakamoto and Kazuo Shinohara, these younger Japanese architects tend toward a diagrammatic reductiveness in their designs. The results range from astonishing geometric elegance to deliberately awkward "dirty realism," but in each case, the buildings are intended to manifest their generating diagrams with a minimum of embellishment.

The work of FOBA, by contrast, uses diagrams as a means of elaboration rather than reduction, intuitively merging programmatic and contextual influences. In an attempt to reveal the spatial variety contained within the visual homogeneity of urban Japan, each design translates the immanent organization of a given locale into architectural form. The goal is to distill and condense the wider context into a single building, while simultaneously having an influence (however minor or modest) beyond the immediate site boundaries.

Each of the projects presented in this book is an outcome of its particular environment: Aura is the brutal compression of the city core; Pleats is the permissive expansion of the countryside; Porous is the incomplete integration of the suburbs; Strata is the implantation of urban complexity in a devastated neighborhood; Skip is the fine-grained web of the traditional city; Stack is the mute juxtaposition of the contemporary metropolis; Organ is the ragged incompletion of the urban periphery;

Myougei is the mutual reinforcement of old and new; Asphodel is a neutral void within urban intensity; Orient is the autonomous abstraction of virtual space; the FOB Homes system engages the inevitable monotony of suburban sprawl.

Although the results may appear sculptural, or even expressionist, the intent is not so much the addition of an aesthetic component to pragmatic requirements as the discovery of alternative ways to organize and inhabit space: software, not art. And contextual in every sense *except* aesthetic.

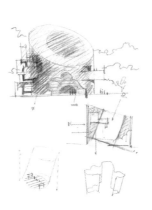

Clarity and Complexity /

Michael Webb

Many architects pursue consistent themes that can be adjusted to any site or building type, while others take a fresh approach to every project, giving each a distinctive expression. FOBA, the firm that Katsu Umebayashi established on the outskirts of Kyoto in 1994, has a foot in both camps. Continuity of space and respect for context are always evident, but the forty-year-old architect eschews a signature style or concept. "I always want to try something unconventional," he observes, "otherwise, why take on a job at all? It should be new every time."

There is no clear line of development from which one can trace a steady evolution of form and language in FOBA's work. From its debut to the present, the firm displays a mastery of problem solving and an eagerness to turn every limitation into an opportunity.

Each project has its own unique character and descriptive name, which are as varied as the sites and the needs of the owners. These names—Aura, Porous, Pleats, and Skip, for example—have an expressive poetry far removed from the cryptic "M-House" and "Y-House" designations that are commonly used in Japan to identify projects without disclosing the location or the name of the owner. FOBA distills the essence of each building into a single word, which then becomes a member of its growing family.

FOBA's buildings respond to the physical constraints or freedoms of a specific site and to the contradictory desires of the owners for openness and enclosure, intimacy and distance. That mixture of objective and subjective conditions is filtered through dialog with the client. At the start of each job, the project architect will not visit the site without first hearing the owners explain why they want to live there and how. In describing the location, the clients reveal aspects of themselves and the elements that concern them the most.

Umebayashi then makes his own evaluation of the site and begins sketching ideas. Though he has no drawing board or computer, and may be directly involved only at the beginning of a project, his contribution is crucial to its success. Intuitive sketches, in combination with organizational diagrams of the constituent spaces, serve as the basis for the designs. These are then developed by team members in axonometric and perspective drawings by hand and, finally, with a computer. The process is one of exploration that can extend over years and go through multiple iterations, even after client approval of a particular scheme.

"In our work, space—volumetric, dynamic, and continuous—comes first," declares Umebayashi. "The movement of a human body through a building defines the space and connects physical reality to psychological perception." This fusion of aesthetic and sensory experience prompts a comparison with contemporary choreography, which has redefined the language and intentions of dance, as FOBA has done for architecture.

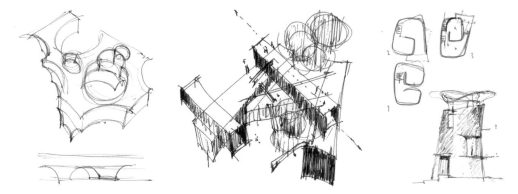

It is instructive to compare FOBA's strategies with those of other contemporary Japanese architects, especially in its home city of Kyoto, where buildings range from discreet wooden rowhouses to garish, misshapen towers—often on adjoining blocks. During the boom years of the 1980s, when extravagance of every kind was prized in Japan, architects went to extremes of showiness and stealth in their buildings. Shin Takamatsu, the Kyoto-based architect with whom Umebayashi spent his formative years, attacked the visual chaos head on with sculptural forms that drew attention to themselves and away from their prosaic neighbors. Fumihiko Maki, the mandarin of minimalism, is responsible for the National Museum of Modern Art in Kyoto (1986), a building that respects the scale of its neighbors but also seems to disdain them. Cool, harmonious, and bloodless, it is a universal building that could have been located anywhere in Japan or abroad.

In contrast to such work, FOBA seeks to engage the urban context—to play to the strengths rather than the weaknesses of the surroundings and to locate the enduring amid the ephemeral. In creating a *pied a terre* (more exactly, a *pied en l'air*) for a copywriter, the architects pitched a tent over a narrow sliver of space in central Tokyo. It was named Aura in reference to the translucent membrane tautly stretched between concrete shear walls, enclosing the two upper levels of flexible living space. It diffuses sunlight by day and glows from within at night, projecting the shadows of its occupants and enriching the drama of the street.

Porous was the name the architects chose to express the interpenetration of space within a house on the northern edge of Kyoto. A notched cube on a tiny corner site, it has been inexpensively clad in corrugated metal that shimmers in the light and unifies the irregular geometry of the architecture. Glass sliders can be retracted on two sides of the open third floor, framing a panorama of roofs and mountains and obliterating the boundary between inside and out.

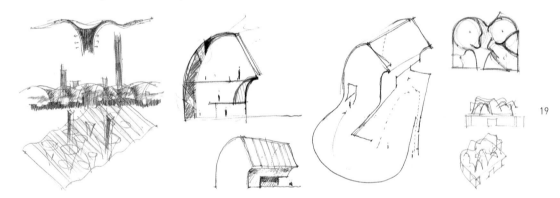

In Kobe, the challenge was to re-create a contextual condition that had been erased by the devastating earthquake of 1995. Strata is a microcosm of the lost neighborhood and an abstraction of the house it replaced. It comprises three concrete cylinders that accommodate the personal needs of different generations of the owner's family, bridged by a wood volume containing shared living and sleeping spaces.

Organ, the first project Umebayashi designed as an independent architect, is both the paradigm of and the home to his practice. Located on a characterless site in Uji, southeast of Kyoto, it comprises two separate but related buildings: Organ 1 is an office that currently houses FOBA's ten architects and Organ 2 is a larger structure for an unrelated engineering company. Many of FOBA's later projects have impassive exteriors that conceal the richness and subtlety of their interior spaces. The Organ complex, by contrast, is a boldly modeled expression of organic volumes: a Rubik's Cube of interlocking boxes, projecting bays, lanterns, and gables, lofted on steel columns and clad in the corrugated metal that is often used for panel trucks. Its pilotis free the ground for parking, visually lighten the structure, and allow it to be viewed from almost any angle.

The complex looks back to Metabolism, a design movement espousing modular construction based on biological metaphors that enjoyed brief notoriety in Japan in the 1960s and 1970s. The Organ complex hints at the megastructures and plug-in capsules of Kenzo Tange and Kisho Kurokawa but seems less the product of industry than of craft—a one-off, hand-made assemblage of simple geometric forms with a clear separation between the metallic skin and the inset wood frames. Its interior resembles a concourse with open spaces eddying off, twisting and rising through a promenade from one end of the building to the other.

While Porous may easily be read as a fragment or miniature of Organ, the Stack house also derives from this early spatial experiment, albeit in a less obvious way.

Its three levels are distinctly articulated as boxes clad in stone and aluminum with raw structural concrete exposed at the lowest level. Each box is slightly offset from the others, generating interstitial openings that animate the interior, and imparting dynamism to what could have been a static composition. Although inspired by the chaotic jumble of the Tokyo townscape, in which buildings are seemingly piled up at random, the forms also give the house the calm authority to withstand the assault of unsightly neighbors and the ever-present ganglia of overhead wires. The external appearance of the house expresses the pent-up energy and the compression of lives and activities in a great metropolis.

Inside, the three levels are linked by vertical cuts that pull natural light from lanterns and clerestories into the center of the house. Eduardo Chillida, the Basque sculptor of interlocking forms, was one inspiration for the cutaway geometry of the interior. The slippages between the levels allow windows to be set back within high parapets, shielded from the street yet permitting views over the city. Operable glass walls link the living room to an adjacent terrace, while translucent and mirrored glass panels are employed to diffuse and reflect natural light and to enhance the sense of spaciousness. In contrast to these airy, light-filled volumes, the wavy ribbed-wood ceiling, wood-paneled wall storage, and subdued lighting of the lower-level office all pay homage to Alvar Aalto's womblike interiors.

The Skip house in northern Kyoto presents an equally enigmatic face to the street: a white concrete box, lofted above a carport and broken only by a thin ribbon of windows and a single porthole to one side. Narrow concrete stairs lead up from within the house and broad wood-tread steps from behind the main gate. They provide complementary routes through and over the multiple levels of the building and meet at a roof terrace that looks down to the street and back over tiled roofs and encircling mountains. The exterior steps flow over the house, revealing rooms

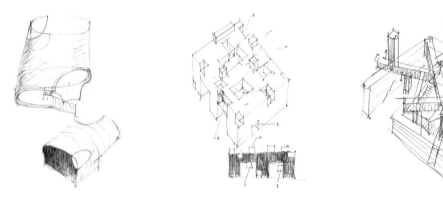

below and to the side, as though the roof has been blown away by a typhoon.

The sense of discovery and intricacy within Skip is as characteristic of traditional Kyoto as Stack's bold massing is of contemporary Tokyo. A former Imperial capital, Kyoto has squandered much of its historic architectural legacy, yet it retains fragments and memories in the form of tiny alleys leading to hidden courtyards, inner gardens, and labyrinthine domestic interiors. FOBA consistently infuses modern architectural forms with traditional Japanese values. Umebayashi grew up in an old Kyoto house and recalls his childhood with deep affection. Unconsciously, perhaps, he has absorbed that sense of tradition into his thinking, creating spiritual oases where old ways can be perpetuated in unabashedly modern settings.

The traditional Japanese interior—with its raised tatami-mat floor, its wall-storage, and absence of furniture—was a multipurpose room where family members learned mutual respect by living, eating, and sleeping all together in the same space. Something was lost when Western customs were adopted and social interaction gave way to a cellular structure in which every person and every activity has its own space. In the Skip house, a traditional room was provided for the elderly uncle and the family shrine, while the teenage son and daughter each have their own retreat, incorporating lofts at the top of the house. Other rooms, however, are shared, and the house has an organic unity, opening up to nature at every point. Even architectural details such as the curving walls and soffits, sliding doors pierced by circular holes, and the *torii*-like roof balustrade evoke the past without mimicking it.

The most explicitly Japanese of the firm's houses is Pleats, which, atypically, is located on a rural site in northern Kyoto Prefecture. The clients requested charred-wood exterior siding and a traditional hearth at the center of the interior, as well as living spaces for the husband's mother and for themselves. It provided an opportunity for FOBA to create a house that expands into the landscape, with private rooms

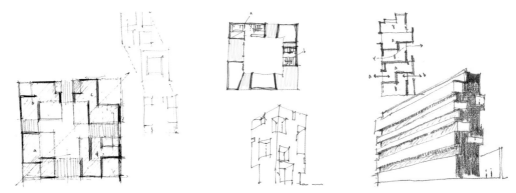

surrounding the central shared space. A diagonal passage from the front door traverses the concentric layers of the house while a square corridor loop cuts straight through the private rooms; the peripheral wall is pleated to enclose little courtyards and areas for gardens. Variations in the floor level provide a consistent low-level framed view of the landscape from sitting and standing positions.

Each of these projects takes a simple idea and explores its potential, achieving complexity with no loss of clarity. In some cases, all the compositional elements fall into place at the outset and remain basically unchanged through the design process; in others, the solution is reached indirectly. At a certain point during the development of Strata, for example, Umebayashi became frustrated by the lack of creative progress and radically changed the design. The clients were alarmed at this shift of direction away from what they had agreed to, but were eventually persuaded that it came closer to what they were searching for without mimicking the house they had lost. Likewise, a full set of construction drawings had been prepared for the Stack house in Tokyo, and the foundations dug, before the clients decided to move to a different site, and commissioned a new set of variations on the original theme.

In these houses and offices, in a *machiya* (traditional townhouse) remodeled to serve as a craft gallery, and in a sleek steel-and-glass art gallery added to a venerable teahouse in the Gion neighborhood of Kyoto, FOBA has shown itself to be as fecund in invention as it is respectful of context. Like other younger Japanese architects—notably Hitoshi Abe, Jun Aoki, Shigeru Ban, and Kengo Kuma—Katsu Umebayashi has found exciting ways to address cramped sites, open up interiors in subtle or dramatic ways, and draw on a legacy of architecture, space planning, and urbanism that many of his predecessors had ignored or swept aside. FOBA is excelling in a country that is hobbled by bureaucratic regulation and degraded by reckless speculation, achieving a satisfying mix

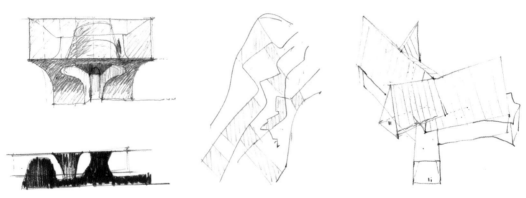

of originality and practicality, surprise and serenity. Each of its buildings is one-of-a-kind and an integral part of a larger whole; the firm's influence is sure to grow as its practice expands in scale, and beyond Japan.

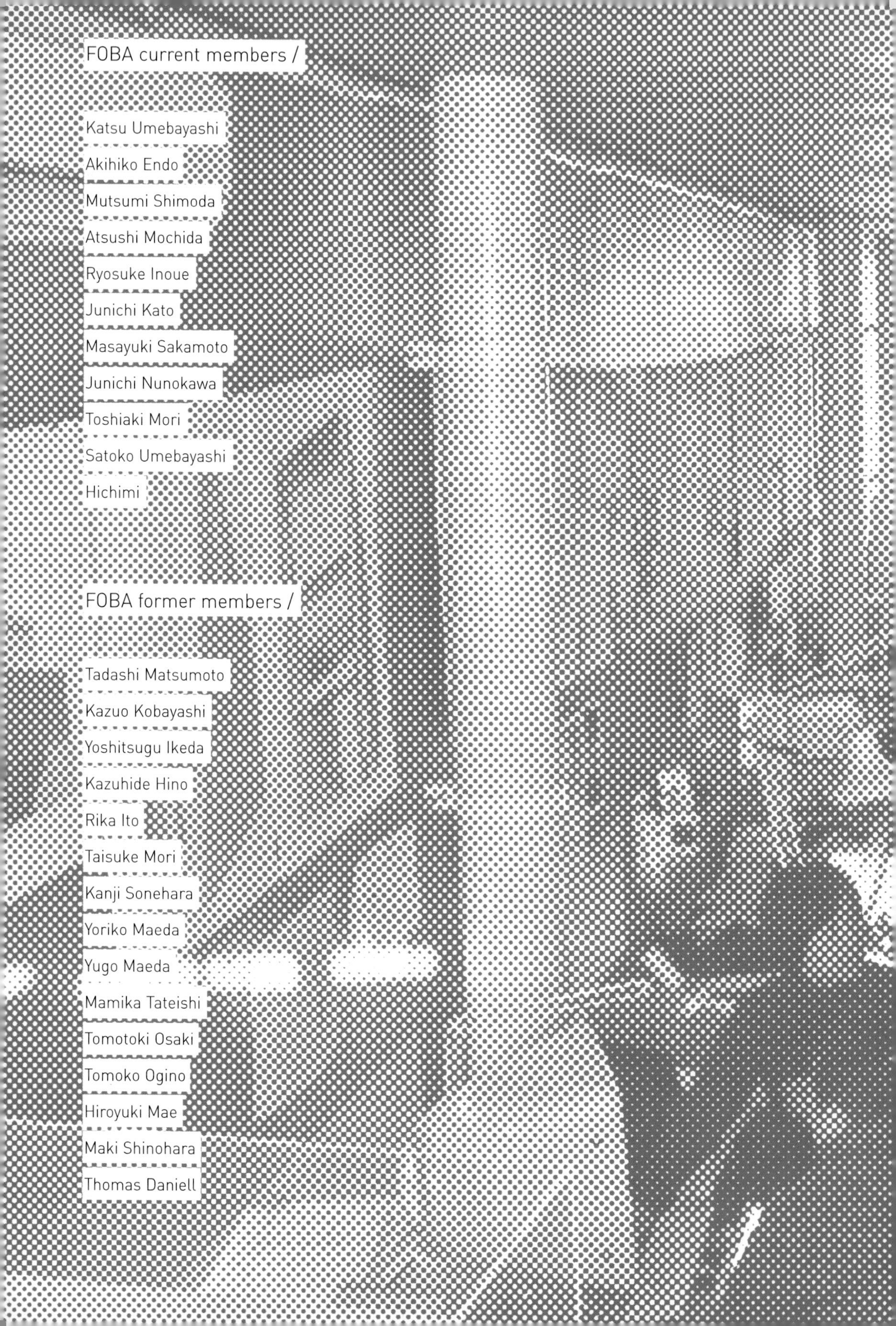

FOBA current members /

Katsu Umebayashi

Akihiko Endo

Mutsumi Shimoda

Atsushi Mochida

Ryosuke Inoue

Junichi Kato

Masayuki Sakamoto

Junichi Nunokawa

Toshiaki Mori

Satoko Umebayashi

Hichimi

FOBA former members /

Tadashi Matsumoto

Kazuo Kobayashi

Yoshitsugu Ikeda

Kazuhide Hino

Rika Ito

Taisuke Mori

Kanji Sonehara

Yoriko Maeda

Yugo Maeda

Mamika Tateishi

Tomotoki Osaki

Tomoko Ogino

Hiroyuki Mae

Maki Shinohara

Thomas Daniell

An ambiguous boundary isolates a space in the central city, thereby creating a provisional privacy and enabling new activities.

Aura /

In central Tokyo, a house requires few domestic facilities. To eat, one goes
to a restaurant; to bathe, the *sento* (public baths); to exercise, the gym;
to be entertained, the cinema. The ultimate Tokyo house is somehow
like an art gallery: an empty, inward-focused space, suffused with filtered
natural light.

Aura is located in a typically narrow and deep urban site—referred
to in Japan as an "eel's nest"—an alley approximately 12 feet (4 meters)
wide by 68 feet (21 meters) long. The challenge was bringing light and air
into the center of the house. We wanted to maximize natural illumination
and potential floor area without resorting to the traditional *tsubo-niwa*
(inner courtyard garden). The site is framed by two longitudinal concrete
walls, connected by cylindrical concrete beams, with a Teflon-coated
fiberglass membrane stretched between them. The translucent roof surface
has a double curvature to sustain tension in the fabric. This was achieved
by giving the two concrete walls identical profiles but opposite orientations.
The roof beams change in angle along the length of the building in order
to connect these two profiles—despite appearances, a rational structural
solution. The fabric skin filters sunlight by day and glows at night: the
building pulses, "breathing" light with the twenty-four-hour rhythm of the
city. Privacy, but no program. Space, but no form.

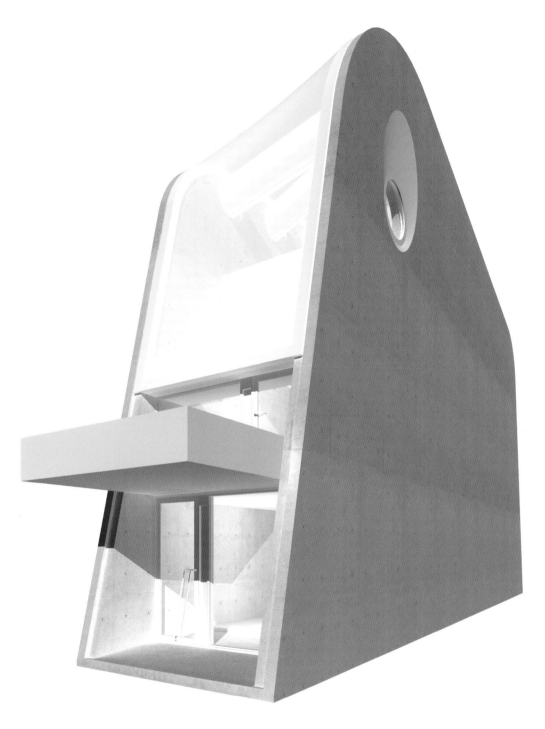

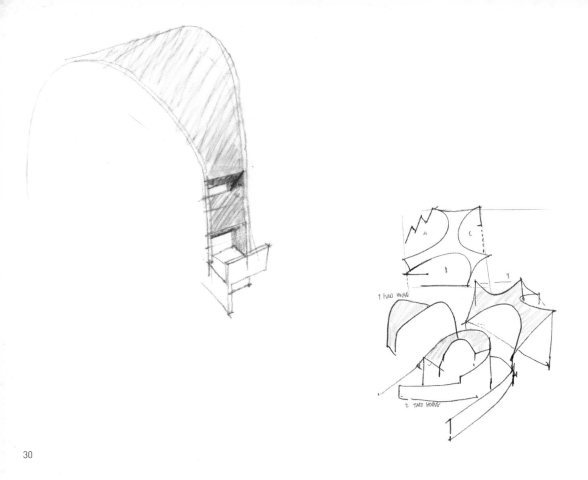

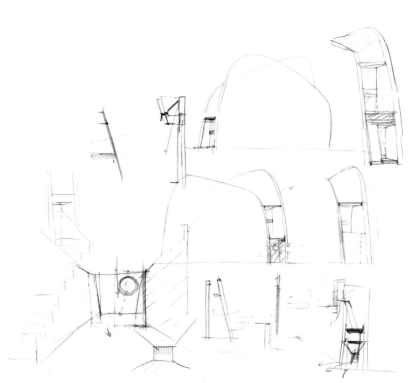

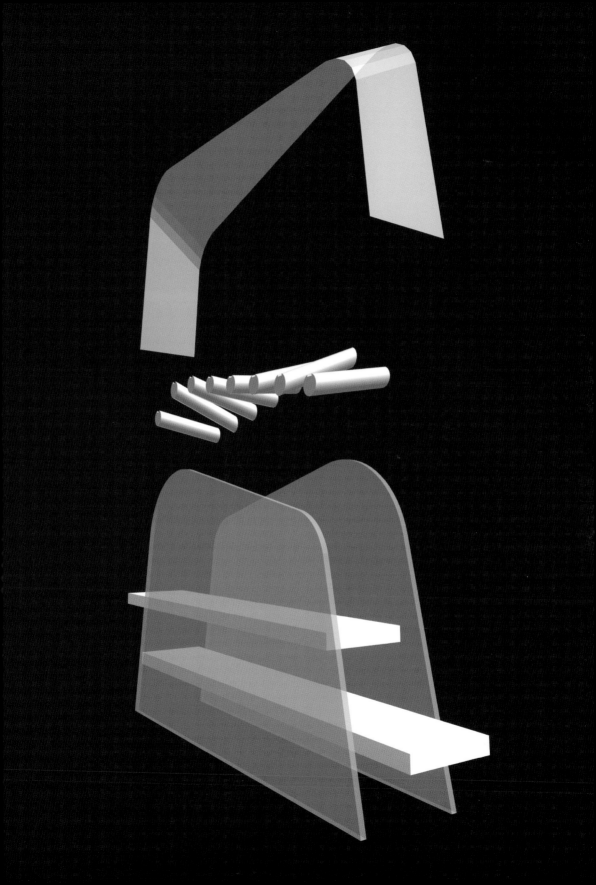

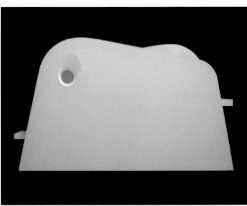

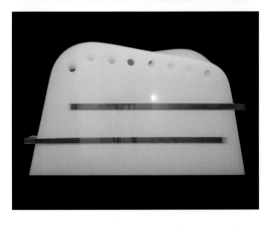

37

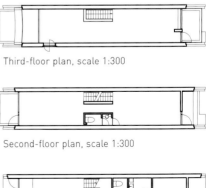

Third-floor plan, scale 1:300

Second-floor plan, scale 1:300

First-floor plan, scale 1:300

Program / office and house

Location / Nishi-azabu, Tokyo

Structure / reinforced concrete

Total floor area / 1,315 square feet (122 square meters)

Site area / 832 square feet (77 square meters)

Design period / May 1994–March 1995

Construction period / November 1995–March 1996

Contractor / Kimi Kensetsu

A supple boundary surface between
the interior and the exterior

Pleats /

Located near the Japan Sea coast in northern Kyoto Prefecture, Pleats
occupies a rural setting with light, air, and views available on all sides.
Without immediate neighbors, the house is able to expand toward adjacent
gardens and distant landscapes. Planned around an *irori* (a traditional
indoor cooking hearth set into the floor), the house was conceived as an
asymmetrical set of nested boxes: a shared space in the middle, storage
and circulation in the intermediate layer, and individual rooms on the
periphery. Horizontal light shafts cutting diagonally across the centripetal
plan bring natural light to the core and link the center to the periphery.
Traditional Japanese houses are organized in a sequence of increasing
privacy and intimacy as one moves deeper into them (the principle of *oku*).
Pleats inverts that relationship: the entry is a "tunnel" leading directly
into the shared space at the heart of the house from which one moves
outward to the personal areas. The private rooms are interposed between
the exterior gardens and the daily living space. Spatially and formally,
Pleats is like a plant inundated with sun and nutrients.

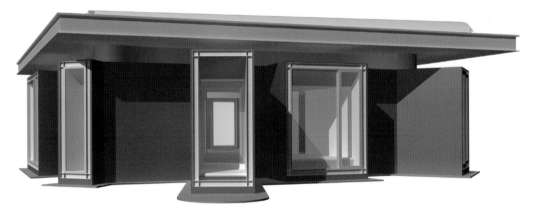

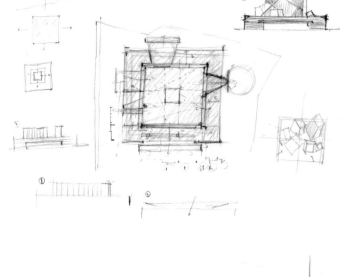

44

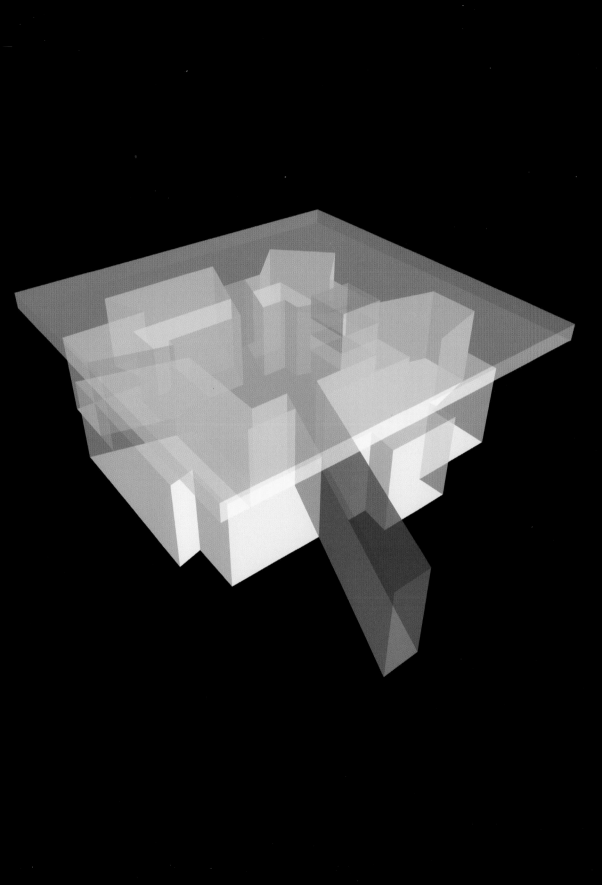

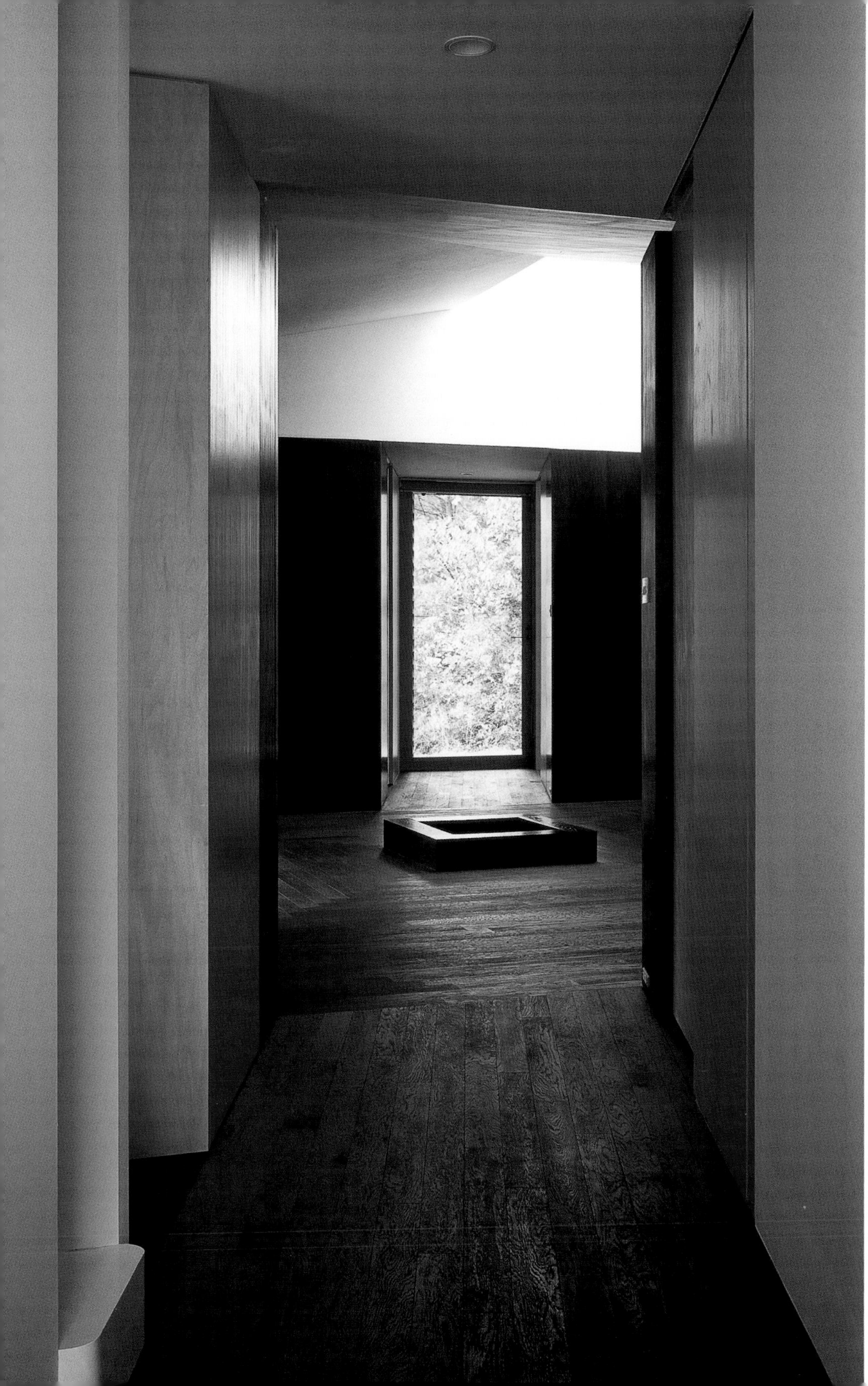

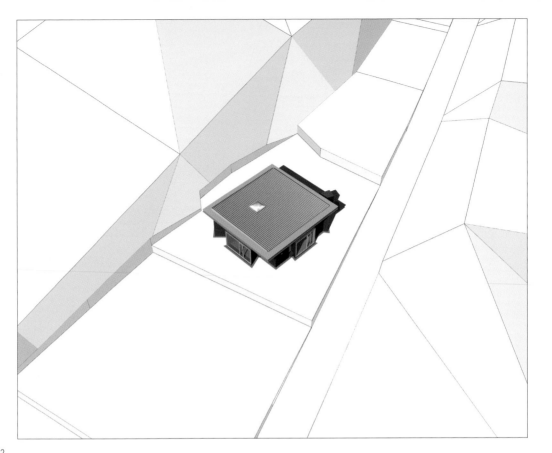

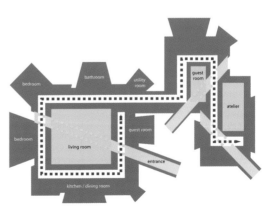

Possible future growth

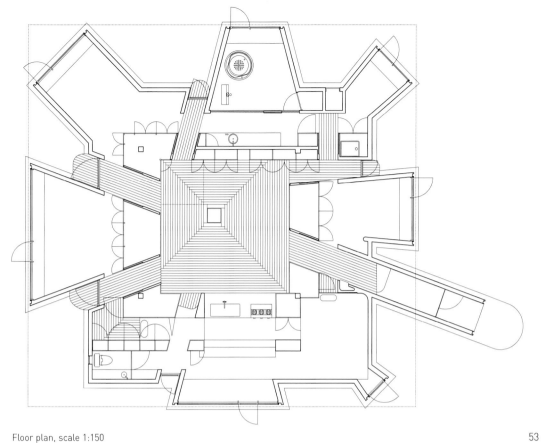

Floor plan, scale 1:150

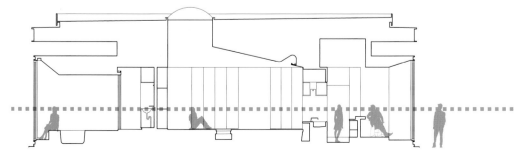

Variations in floor level create a consistent eye level across the building.

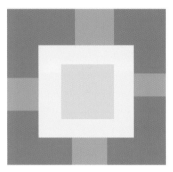

Alignment with exterior context
Superimpositon of light tunnels

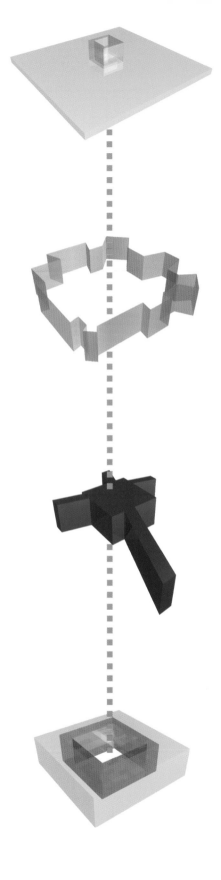

54

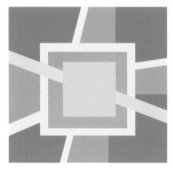

Secondary spatial zoning
Links between layers

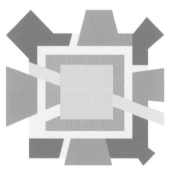

Entry and circulation path
Pleating of exterior wall planes

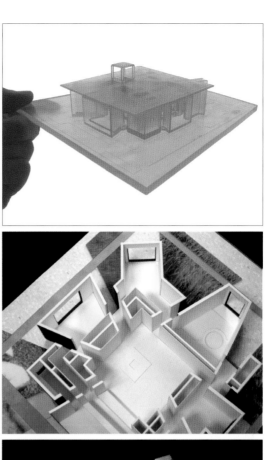

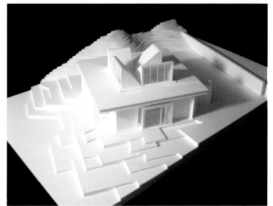

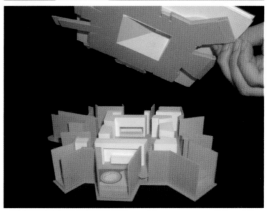

Program / single-family house

Location / Mineyama, Kyoto

Structure / steel

Total floor area / 2,063 square feet (192 square meters)

Site area / 9,977 square feet (927 square meters)

Design period / December 1998–April 1999

Construction period / March 2000–October 2000

Contractor / Shimizu Komuten

"Notched" space allowing the integration of
inside and outside

Porous /

On the northern side of Kyoto, the city abruptly ends where a mountain range begins. The urban edge is a patchwork of solid and void: private residences scattered among tiny rice fields, vegetable gardens, and vacant lots.

A small house for a young couple, Porous optimizes its restricted site by means of spatial connectivity across its four levels. Local regulations limit both the overall height and total floor area; maximizing the building envelope would have resulted in more floor area than is legally permitted. The solution was to make an array of large openings in the walls and floors, decreasing the total surface area, and reducing the divisions between individual rooms. This results in three-dimensional continuous spaces across adjacent levels. Externally, it is a metal-clad cubic volume with large notches carved from it. Internally, these notches overlap like an Eduardo Chillida sculpture. In certain places, the interior spaces swell beyond the building volume and engage the surrounding environment. Daylight enters from unexpected directions; there are no dark corners. The experiential consequence of these simple gestures is a psychological spaciousness far greater than the actual floor area should allow. Instead of small, isolated rooms, the spaces blend into one another as the entire house merges with its context.

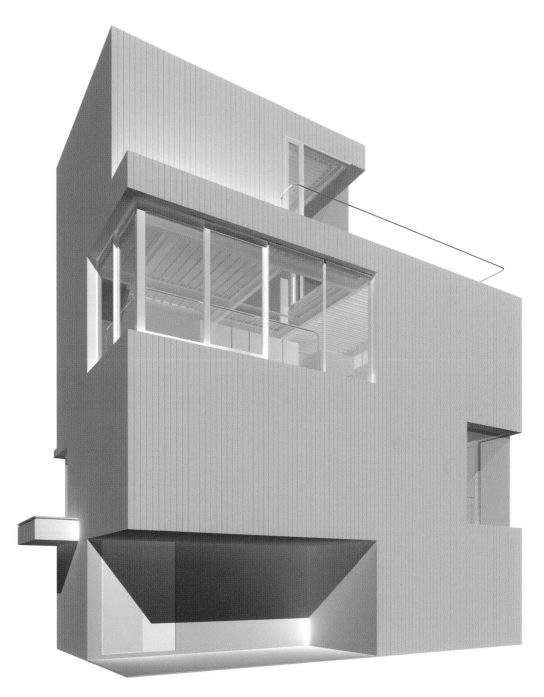

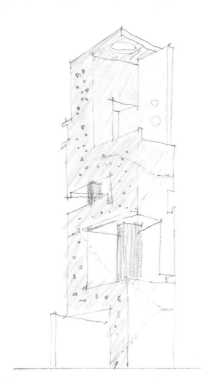

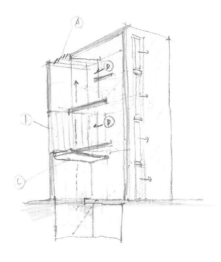

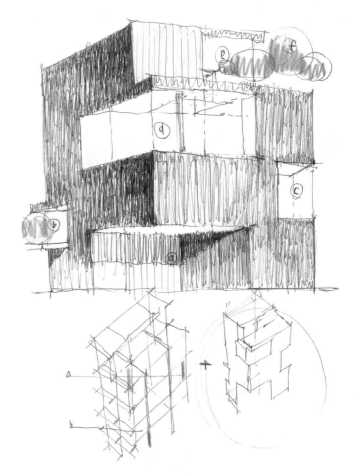

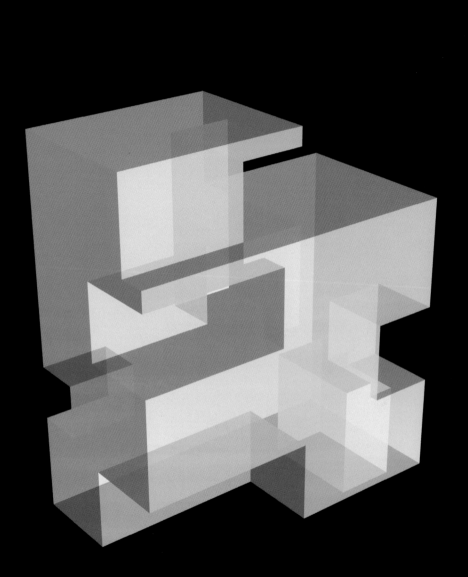

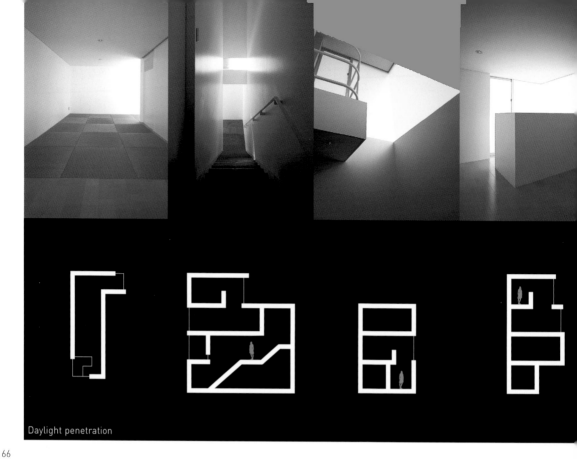

Daylight penetration

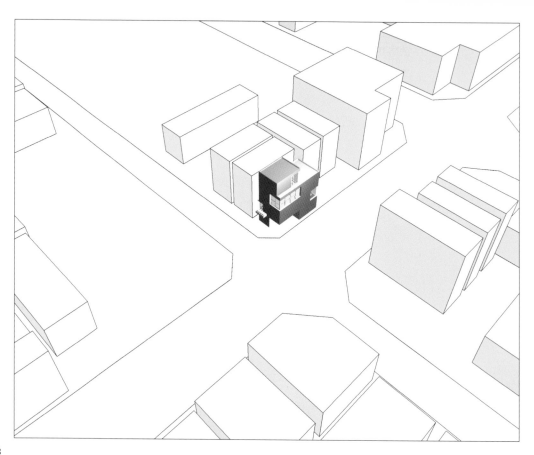

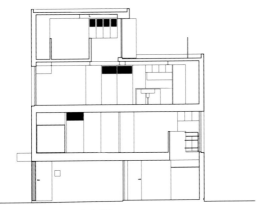

Section, scale 1:200

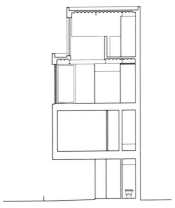

Section, scale 1:200

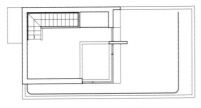

Fourth-floor plan, scale 1:200

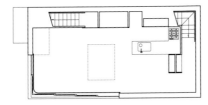

Third-floor plan, scale 1:200

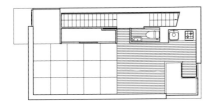

Second-floor plan, scale 1:200

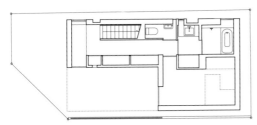

First-floor plan, scale 1:200

Program / single-family house

Location / Kitayama, Kyoto

Structure / steel

Total floor area / 1,435 square feet (133 square meters)

Site area / 746 square feet (69 square meters)

Design period / February 2002–June 2002

Construction period / July 2002–January 2003

Contractor / E.S.T. Corporation

A city decimated by an earthquake then rebuilt
with bland, generic buildings

Strata /

Strata was commissioned to replace a large traditional house in a residential area that was almost completely destroyed by the February 1995 Kobe earthquake and then quickly rebuilt with generic suburban houses. At the most abstract level, a city may be considered to be an accumulation of disparate elements, the proximity and juxtaposition of which creates vitality and interest. Here, the intricate historical city texture has been lost; the new house must therefore generate an urban synergy within itself.

 The entire site was treated as a garden, throughout which three independent concrete cylinders—private spaces for different generations of a single family—were dispersed, with a shared wooden volume placed on top. Large translucent acrylic tubes pass vertically through the upper volume, providing natural light to the lower level; at night, the cylinders are artificially lit from within. A number of small glass pavilions (tea rooms) were proposed for the top of the wooden box, but they remain unbuilt. These primary components are stacked in layers without apparent structural, formal, or functional relationships; their simplicity as objects is countered by their complexity as an ensemble. Strata was conceived as a kind of microurbanism, an enclave of density and intensity within a banal suburban context.

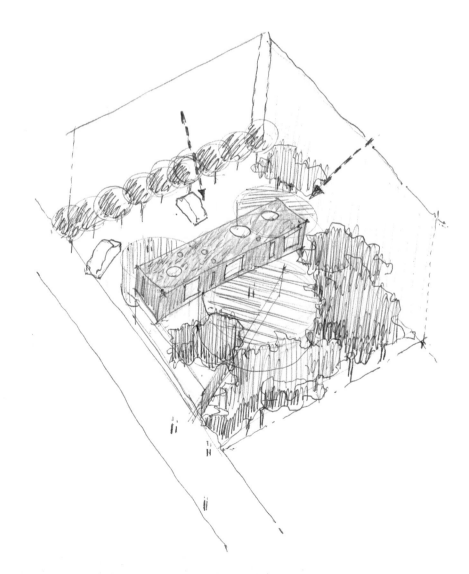

HOUSE B

HOUSE C

HOUSE A

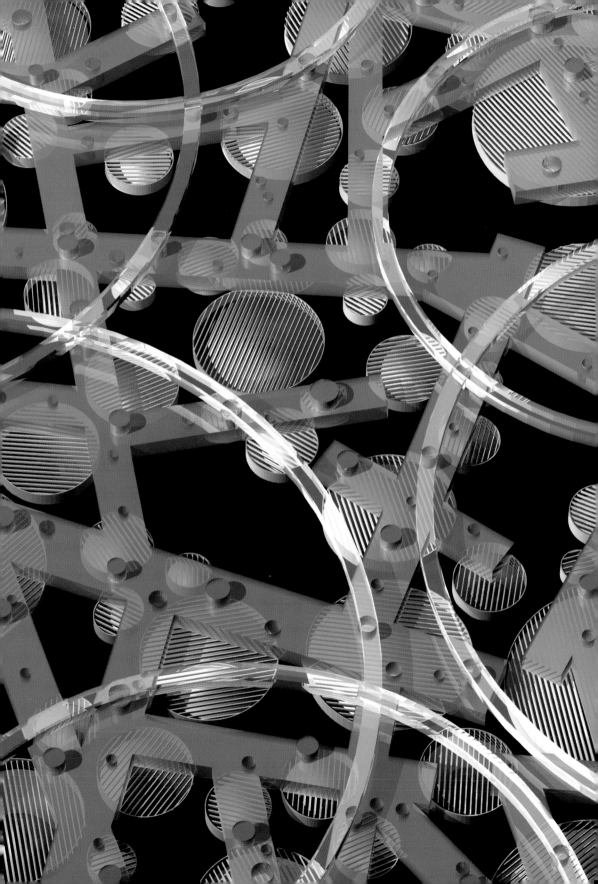

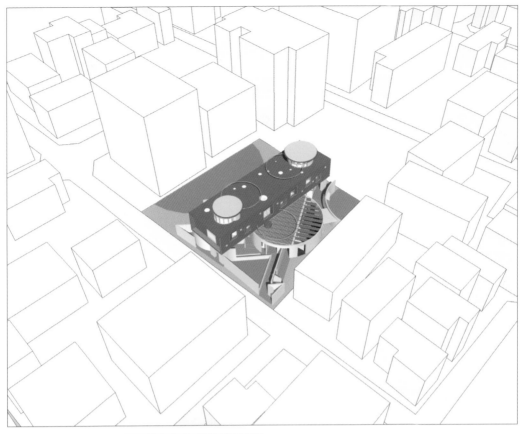

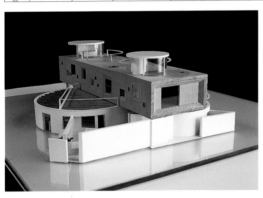

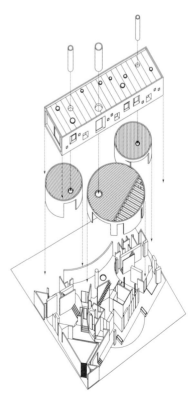

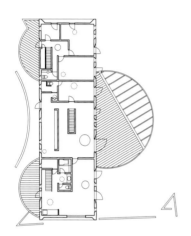

Second-floor plan, scale 1:400

First-floor plan, scale 1:400

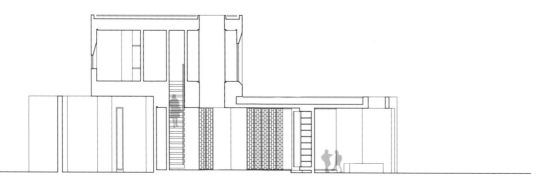

Section, scale 1:200

Program / multigeneration house

Location / Uozaki, Kobe

Structure / reinforced concrete (first floor), timber (second floor)

Total floor area / 5,316 square feet (494 square meters)

Site area / 5,360 square feet (498 square meters)

Design period / October 1995–November 1996

Construction period / January 1997–April 1998

Contractor / Nakanishi Kensetsu

A city comprising an intricate
network of paths and gardens

Skip /

The city of Kyoto is a network of paths and gardens bounded by mountain ranges. The urban experience is an intricate web of picturesque variety, permeable and continuous. Skip is a microcosm of the city—a miniature of Kyoto's spatial structure. The clients requested the largest possible garden area, so the entire upper surface of the building became an accessible outdoor terrace. Rather than a floating Corbusian roof deck, however, it takes the form of a wide stair that begins at ground level, rises to the rear of the site, and then turns back to reach the uppermost terrace. From the street, Skip is a modernist box. From the rear, it is a picturesque garden. From the air, it blends comfortably with the tiled roofs and courtyard gardens of the surrounding neighborhood. Like Adalberto Libera's Casa Malaparte, Skip is simultaneously a discrete object and an extension of the contours of its site—less a building than a landscape. Unlike Casa Malaparte, the circulation is a loop, linked to the street and integrated with the city—more a path than a container. Both floating above the site and anchored in the bedrock, Skip was conceived as a solid mass from which inhabitable spaces have been carved: a jigsaw of exterior canyons and interior caverns.

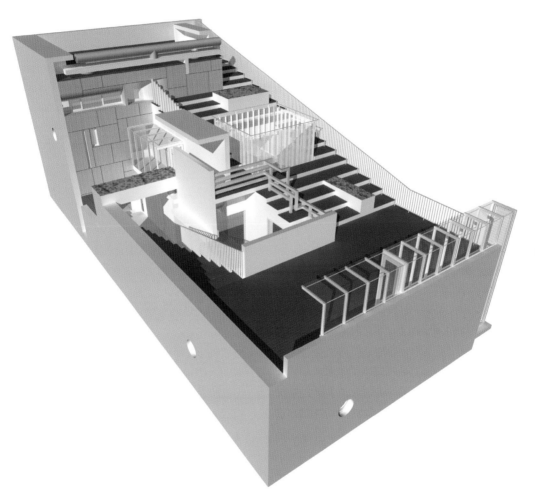

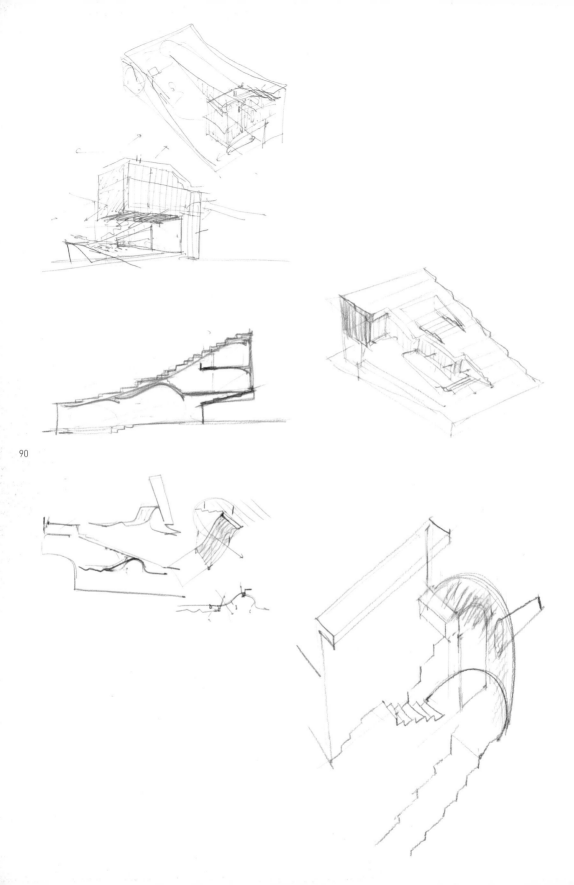

90

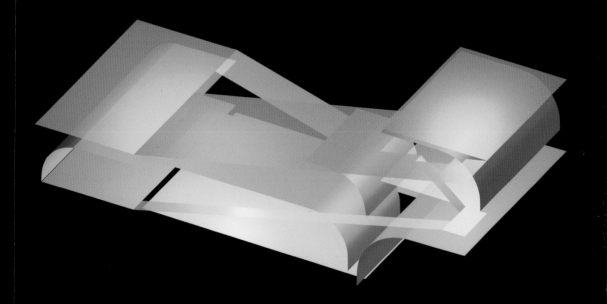

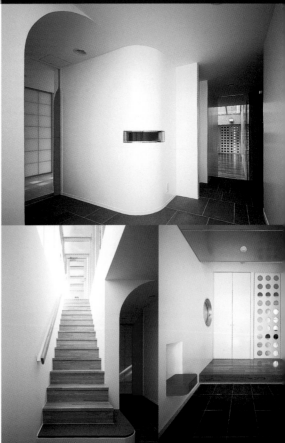

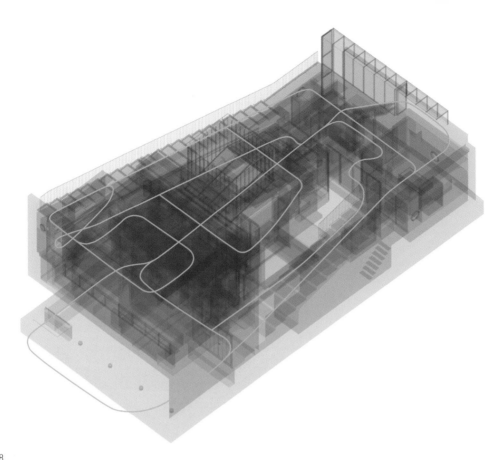

98

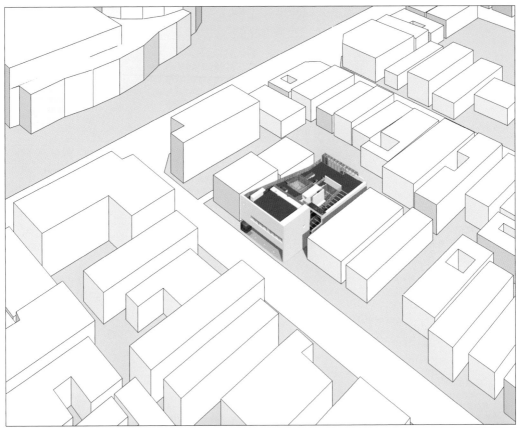

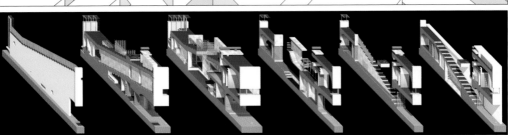

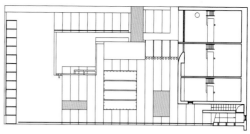

Loft-level plan, scale 1:350

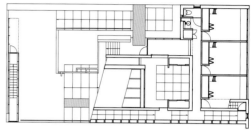

Second-floor plan, scale 1:350

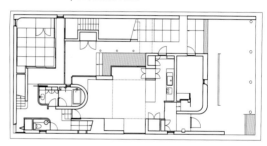

First-floor plan, scale 1:350

Lateral sections, scale 1:350

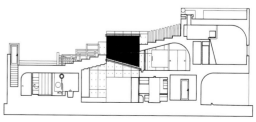

Longitudinal section, scale 1:350

Program / single-family house

Location / Shimogamo, Kyoto

Structure / reinforced concrete

Total floor area / 2,483 square feet (231 square meters)

Site area / 3,104 square feet (288 square meters)

Design period / November 1998–October 1999

Construction period / November 2001–October 2002

Contractor / Nihon Kokudo Kaihatsu

Urban context composed from the blunt juxtaposition of unrelated elements

Stack /

In the amorphous complexity of central Tokyo, the scale of the city's organization is too vast to be perceived by the pedestrian observer. At street level, urban form is either incoherent or irrelevant; the Tokyo experience is a succession of interior spaces. The city appears to consist of mute volumes, their only apparent relationship one of simple adjacency.

Located near Yoyogi Park in central Tokyo, Stack is Tokyo urbanism in microcosm. From the outside, it is a haphazard stack of three boxes clad in different materials: concrete, stone, aluminum. Internally, vertical voids connect and complicate the three levels. Although the house seems to be sealed off from its surroundings, the closure is incomplete: spatial and visual connections are maintained through the horizontal and vertical slots that result from "slippage" between the solid volumes. Additional slippage between elements is manifest at every level: long and narrow courtyard gardens result from the misalignment of the boxes, handrails transform from incisions to protrusions as they pass between layers, walls delaminate at their edges; boxes nest within boxes, corners are misaligned. These abrupt juxtapositions are balanced by the subtle visual links created by light shafts carved through the functional spaces within the house, and between the house interior and the exterior environment. Life occurs in the interstices.

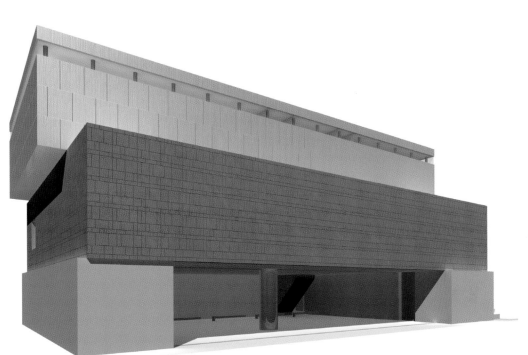

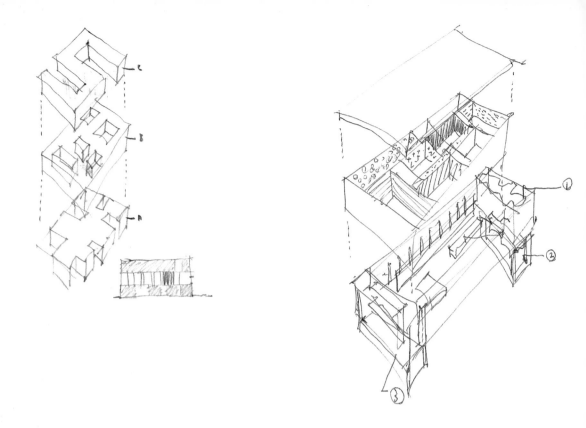

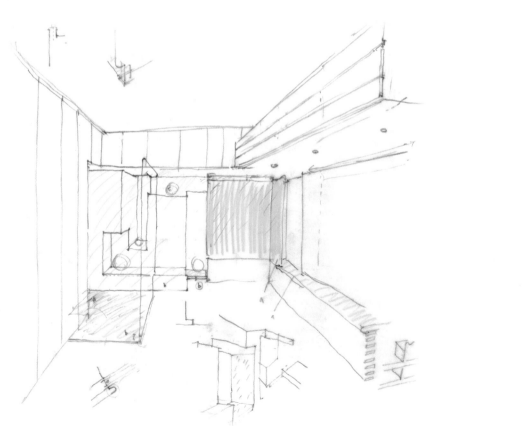

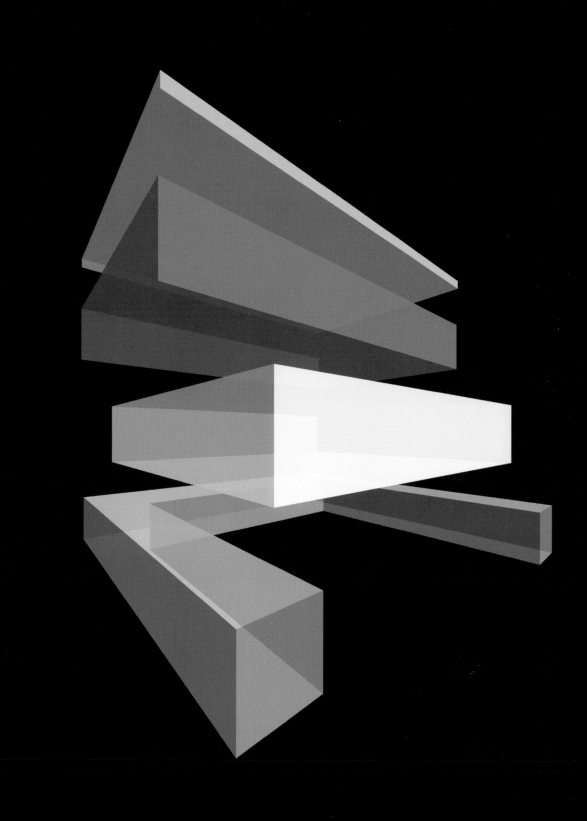

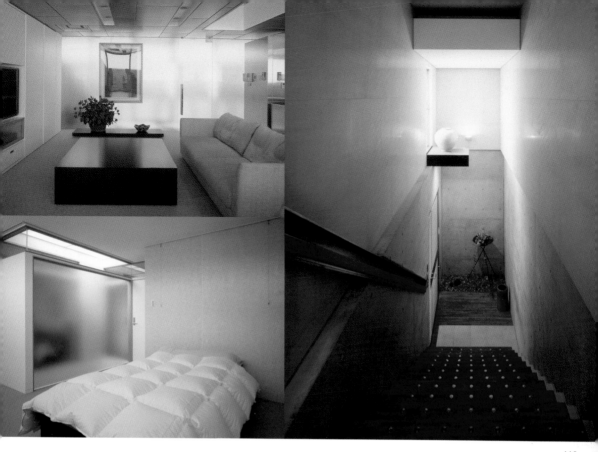

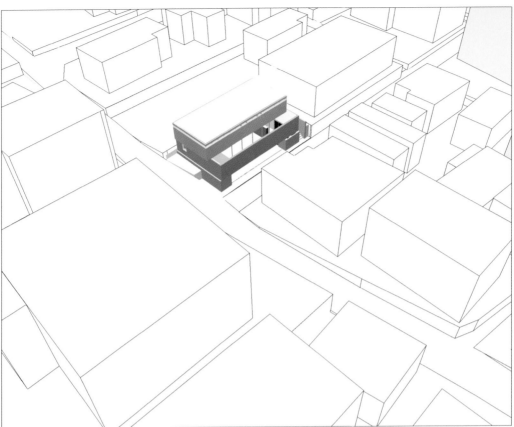

Composition = Stacking

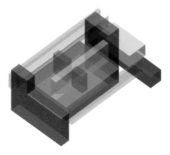

Relationship = Proximity

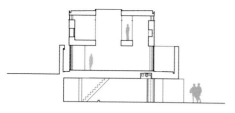

Section, scale 1:350

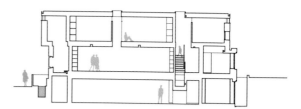

Section, scale 1:350

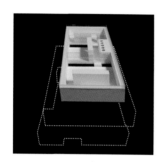

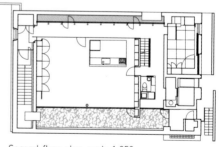

Third-floor plan, scale 1:350

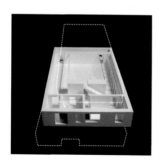

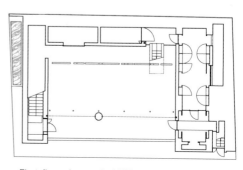

Second-floor plan, scale 1:350

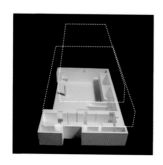

First-floor plan, scale 1:350

Program / single-family house

Location / Yoyogi, Tokyo

Structure / reinforced concrete (first and second floor), steel (third floor)

Total floor area / 5,114 square feet (475 square meters)

Site area / 2,481 square feet (231 square meters)

Design period / August 1998–January 1999

Construction period / February 1999–August 1999

Contractor / I. D. International

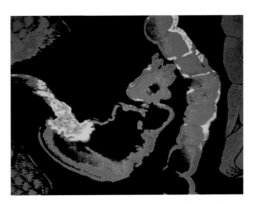

Purely functional requirements leading to the
evolution of complex forms

Organ /

Can an office environment combine spatial variety with pragmatic efficiency? Can functional flexibility be achieved without resorting to the "universal space" of modernism?

Uji City is on the periphery of Kyoto, at the ragged edge where the urban dissolves into the agricultural. Organ 1 (the head office of FOBA) was intended as a prototypical alternative to the homogeneous space of conventional office buildings. It is a single, extendable volume, a rectilinear tube that distorts and inflects in response to both internal (programmatic) and external (contextual) forces. When additional space becomes needed, it may be "extruded" by extending the structure from the ends of the tube. The intent is open-endedness and opportunistic growth—incomplete by definition.

Organ 2 was completed two years later for a firm of structural engineers. Although the two buildings are discontinuous, there is a similar experimentation with spatial continuity and free massing. They are conceived as a single entity comprising a functional interior choreography and complementary exterior spaces—the area among the pilotis is used for parking, parties, and as a meeting point for people in the neighborhood.

The Organ complex can be seen as a synthesis between two of the most interesting avant-garde movements of the last century, Japanese Metabolism and European expressionism—both of which contain undeveloped potential. These projects are an attempt to create Metabolism without megastructure and expressionism without ornament.

122

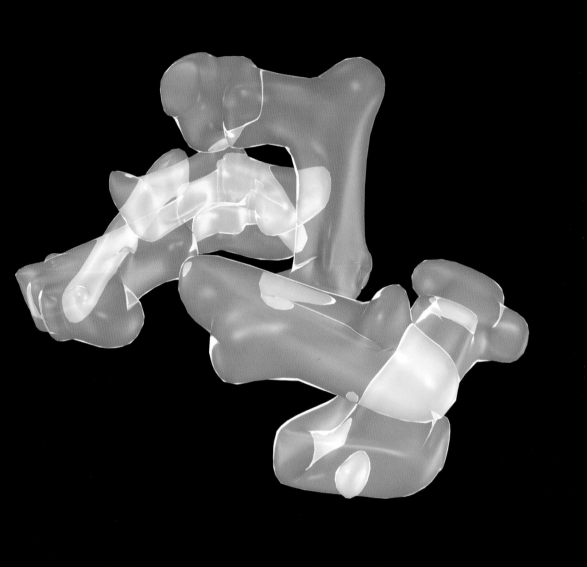

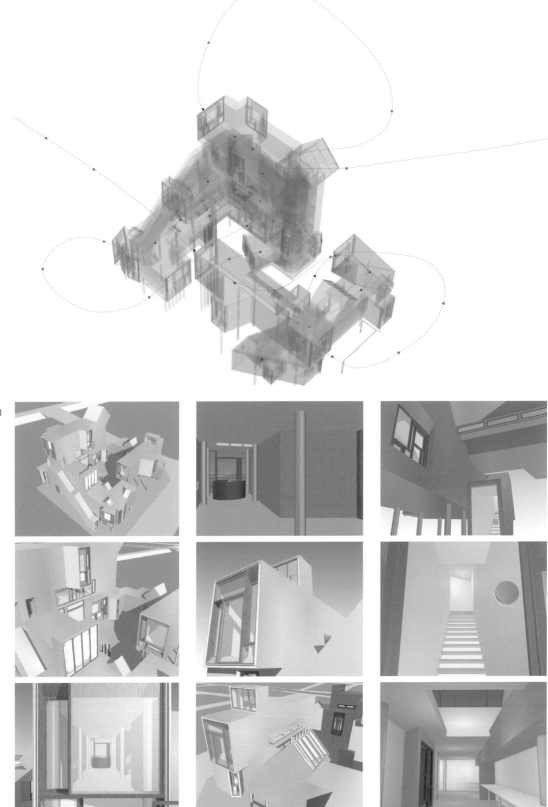

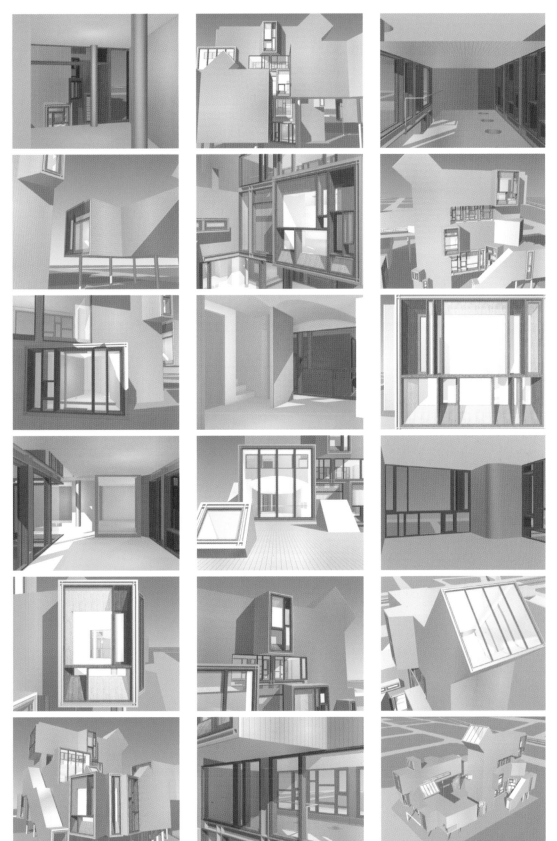

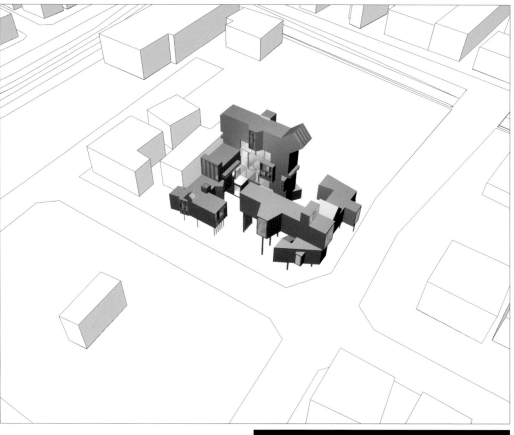

130

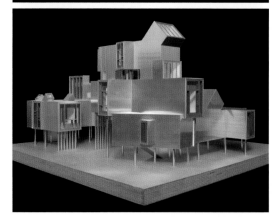

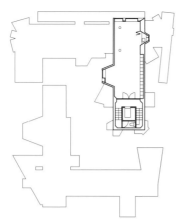

Fifth-floor plan, scale 1:500

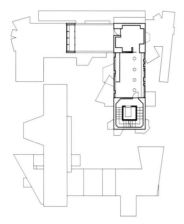

Fourth-floor plan, scale 1:500

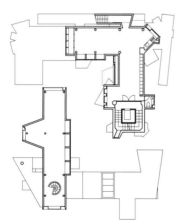

Third-floor plan, scale 1:500

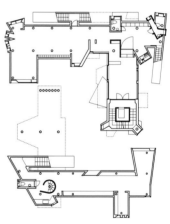

Second-floor plan, scale 1:500

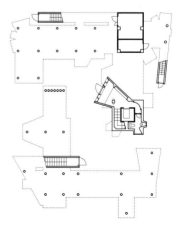

First-floor plan, scale 1:500

ORGAN 1 /

Program / office building

Location / Uji, Kyoto

Structure / steel

Total floor area / 2,831 square feet (263 square meters)

Site area / 6,322 square feet (587 square meters)

Design period / February 1994–November 1994

Construction period / December 1994–June 1995

Contractor / Miyamoto Komuten

ORGAN 2 /

Program / office building

Location / Uji, Kyoto

Structure / steel

Total floor area / 3,601 square feet (335 square meters)

Site area / 2,980 square feet (277 square meters)

Design period / December 1995–April 1996

Construction period / April 1996–September 1997

Contractor / Shimooka Kensetsu

Using fabric to gently separate the spaces

Myougei /

The Imperial capital for a thousand years, Kyoto is unique among Japanese cities for two reasons: it has a recognizable urban structure (an orthogonal grid) and a clear boundary (a surrounding ring of mountains). The city was spared from bombing during the Second World War, only to then lose most of its traditional architecture to economic development over the following decades. Harsh inheritance taxes and inflated land prices decimated the city center. The result is like a photographic negative of the historical European city: rather than a preserved core surrounded by an increasingly dominant modern periphery, the old city of Kyoto has dissolved from the inside out. The past survives as a ragged belt of temples and gardens around the urban perimeter.

    Located on the edge of the city among similar traditional buildings, Myougei was originally a family home. With their children gone, the retired owners decided to convert the front section into an art gallery while maintaining the rear section as a private residence. The basic shell was renovated, and several clearly new elements were inserted. Additional circulation links were created and daylight penetration was enhanced. The street presence comprises a white-framed display window and sliding lattice panels that reference the language of Kyoto's traditional domestic architecture.

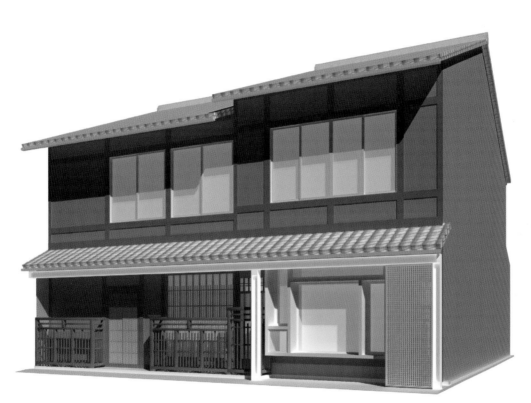

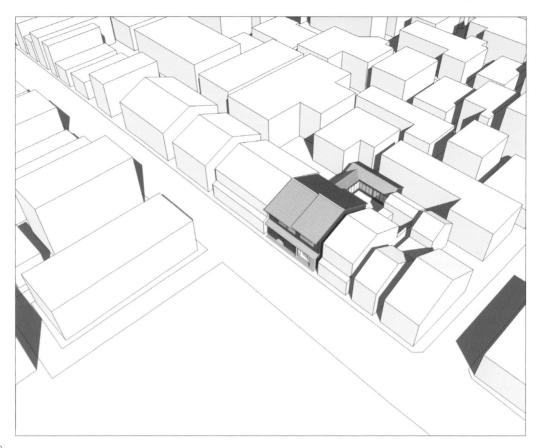

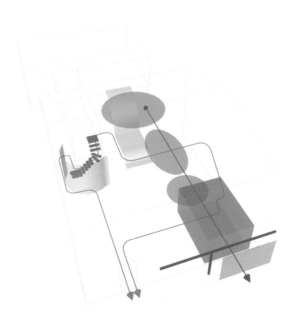

New circulation loop

Second-floor plan, scale 1:300

First-floor plan, scale 1:300

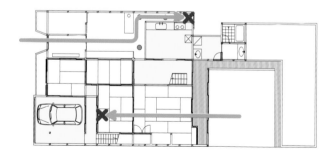

Existing blockages

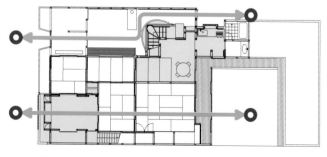

New connections

Program / art gallery and residence

Location / Sakyo, Kyoto

Structure / timber (renovation of existing townhouse)

Total floor area / 846 square feet (79 square meters)

Site area / N/A

Design period / April 1998–August 1998

Construction period / September 1998–June 1999

Contractor / Tokusho Kensetsu

Flexible spaces defined by the
arrangement of mobile planes

Asphodel /

Japan's geisha tradition has all but disappeared; it survives mainly in the teahouses of Kyoto's Gion district. Few people can afford the price of geisha entertainment, and even fewer are interested in studying to become geisha themselves. The quandary for teahouse owners is whether to compromise and modernize or rigorously maintain their traditions. Teahouse buildings are constructed of wood, bamboo, clay, and paper. They require constant maintenance and have limited potential for adaptive reuse.

Asphodel is a contemporary art gallery and private salon commissioned by the daughter of a venerable teahouse-owning family. It functions as an annex to the original teahouse building, which is located on an adjacent street; the two are discreetly linked at the rear of the property. For a gallery with no permanent art collection, a generic "white cube" is the logical solution. The architectural challenge is to achieve a variety of spatial experiences within such a simple interior.

A longitudinally aligned sliding wall on the lowest level can be used to divide the space or create an optional corridor for direct access to the upper levels. Materials varying in opacity, translucency, transparency, and reflectivity contribute to an apparent spatial expansion and compression as one moves through the building. Like the teahouse, it is a space defined by translucent and mobile planes.

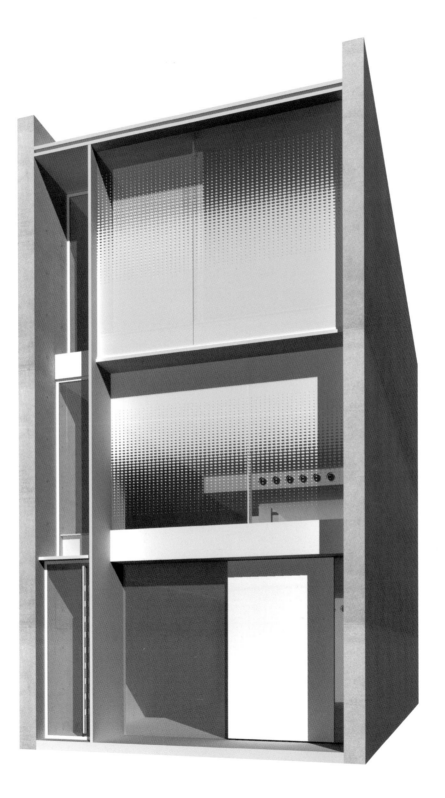

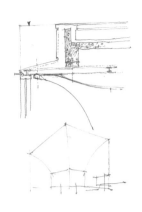

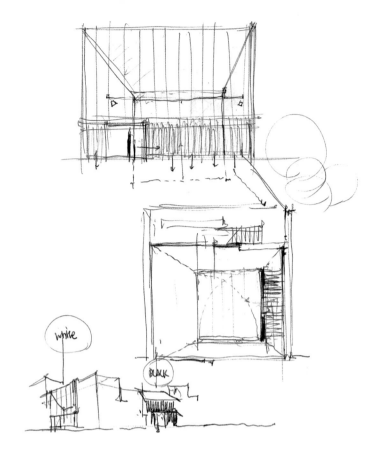

white

BLACK

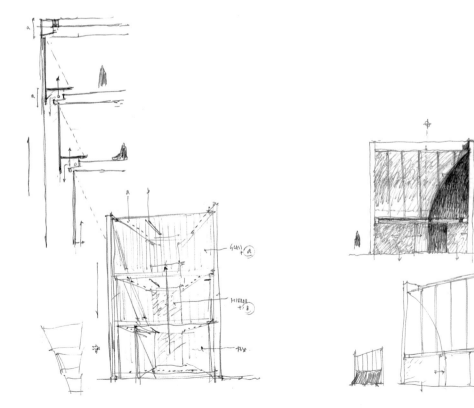

GLASS a

MIRROR
+ B

PLY

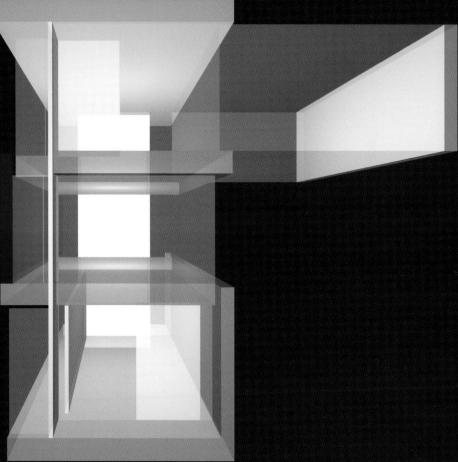

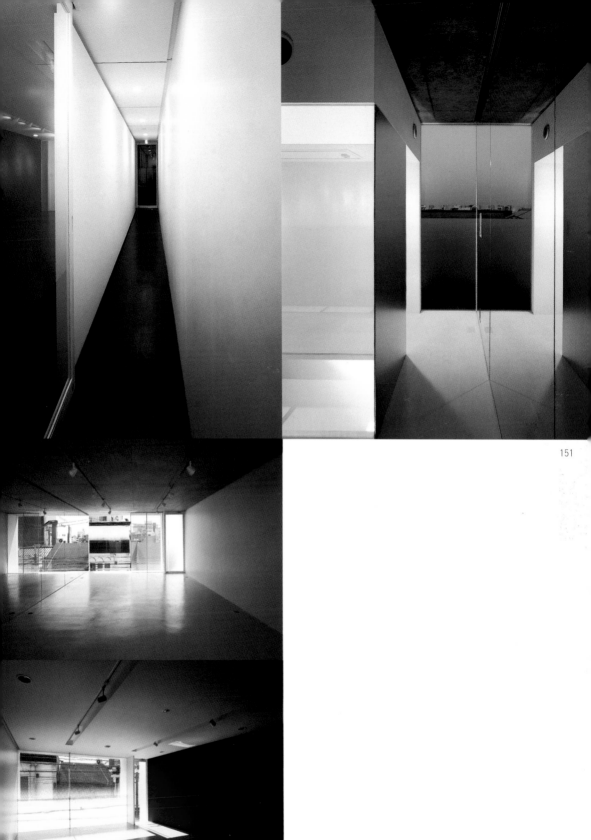

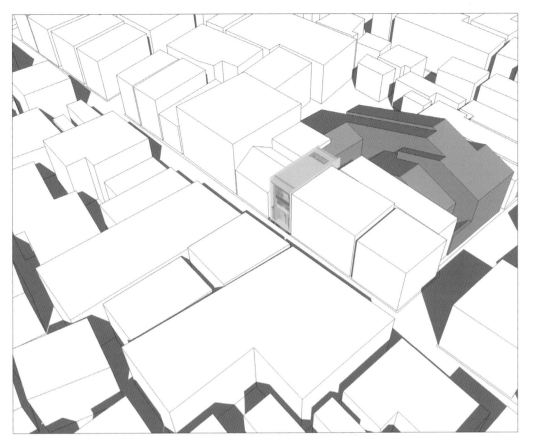

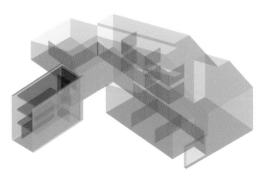

Teahouse-to-gallery connection

Third-floor plan, scale 1:200

Second-floor plan, scale 1:200

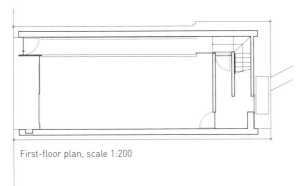

First-floor plan, scale 1:200

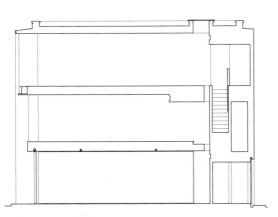

Section, scale 1:200

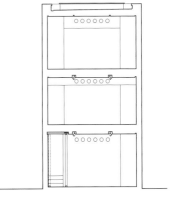

Section, scale 1:200

Program / art gallery and salon
Location / Gion, Kyoto
Structure / reinforced concrete
Total floor area / 2,071 square feet (192 square meters)

Luminous ceiling enclosing a space that is
simultaneously introverted and extroverted

Orient /

Like comparable facilities worldwide, Osaka Port is as much part of a transnational trade infrastructure as it is part of Osaka. Context here is more global and intangible than local and physical. This multipurpose pavilion for Osaka Bay is being developed as a prototype for what is anticipated to become an extensive global network connected by publicly accessible Internet links. The function is undetermined, and the building will be available for temporary hire by clients in both the private and public sectors.

Orient is structured as a stack of solid glass disks with a variety of spaces and pathways excavated from them. Each disk may rotate independently, allowing multiple spatial configurations and circulation routes. Constantly changing images—news, entertainment, advertising, artworks—are projected onto the internal glass surfaces, dematerializing the object and blurring the boundary between form and content. Although the internal space has no fixed shape, at one particular orientation the internal voids align to produce a large pyramidal space. A particular optical effect then results: mutual reflections create the illusion of an enormous sphere floating above observers inside. Solid cylinder, void pyramid, virtual sphere: archaic forms containing virtual spaces.

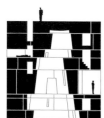

Multimedia projections on glass surfaces

Internal reflections create illusory sphere

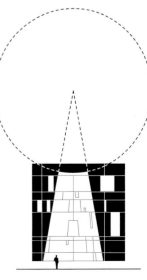

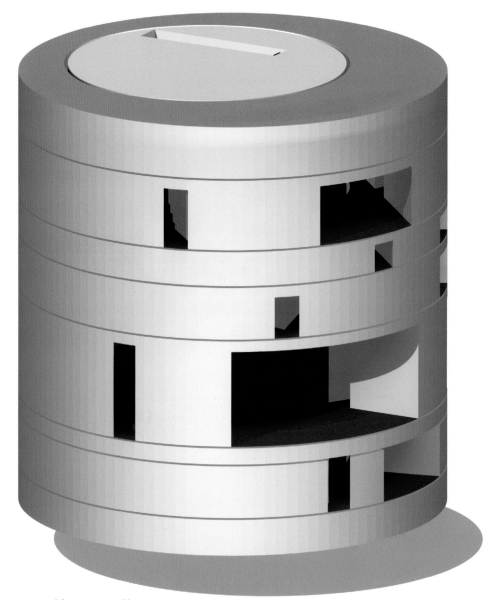

Program / multipurpose pavilion

Location / undetermined

Structure / cast glass

Total floor area / variable

Site area / N/A

Design period / January 1999–February 1999

Construction period / unbuilt

Collaborating artist / Akira Hasegawa

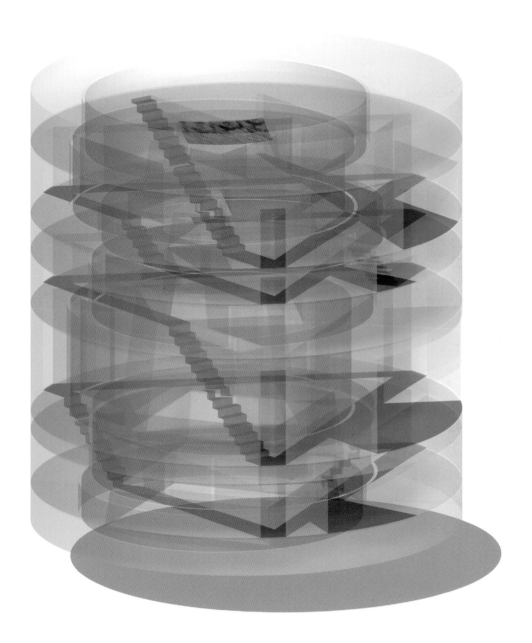

FOB Homes: Brand Recognition /

Thomas Daniell

A significant portion of contemporary residential construction in Japan consists of mass-produced,
prefabricated houses. This is the world of "housemakers": enormous marketing/design/construction
companies such as Misawa Homes, Sekisui House, or
Panahome, which are themselves often divisions of
even larger corporations. The housemaker houses are
based on a set of modular plan typologies, wherein
every detail, fitting, and finish may be selected from
huge catalogs. Their marketing brochures invariably
show Western-style houses isolated among lush
gardens. In reality, they are likely to be framed by
narrow yards, with windows facing directly into their
neighbors' walls. Replacing Japan's traditional
extended-family dwellings, they were first marketed
after the Second World War as the modern home
for the nuclear family. With an intended life span of
only three decades, this is house as consumer item—
conventional, convenient, and disposable.

　　　　While the Western influence is obvious in
details such as the street-facing gable ends and side-
hung windows, it also extends to the internal planning.
The flexibly divided, multipurpose rooms of the traditional house have been replaced with solid walls and
private rooms for each family member. This culturally
alien emphasis on individuality has been identified
as a contributing factor to contemporary juvenile delinquency and the *hikikomori* phenomenon—people who
stay confined to their rooms and avoid human contact.

　　　　Despite the housemakers' phenomenal
success over the last few decades, they are proving

too top heavy and inflexible for recent sociological and demographic shifts. As land prices and the birth rate continue to decline, the perceived purpose of the home has shifted from a family shelter and status symbol to a comfortable retreat for indulging hobbies and entertaining friends. The result is an enormous potential client base dissatisfied with what the housemakers have to offer, yet wary of commissioning an architect—partly due to the profession's (often deserved) reputation for designing houses that are expensive, indulgent, and dysfunctional.

The gap between generic housemaker products and unique architect-designed houses seemed like a niche begging to be filled—both as business proposition and as social vision. In 1999, FOBA established a subsidiary company to provide an alternative housing "brand": FOB Homes. The emphasis

was on marketing and logistics rather than new materials and construction techniques. FOB Homes can be made of anything, made anyhow. It is only the spatial and aesthetic concepts that remain consistent.

Architecturally, the FOB Homes system is based on two principles: spatial continuity throughout the interior and containment of external areas within the main volume. Interlocking L-shaped spaces (allowing every room to disappear around a corner) and courtyard gardens (conceived as roofless rooms) visible throughout the house result in an experiential, if not actual, spaciousness. The lack of clear room divisions and the resulting functional ambiguity is in many ways a return to a more traditional type of house.

Visually, the FOB Home is a solid mass, a hermetic white volume filling its site. The apparent insensitivity to context is, in fact, generosity. The blank external walls effectively "donate" their exterior spaces to the adjacent houses: the neighbors may open their curtains without losing any privacy.

Such austere facades may have upset people in an earlier era, but given the visual chaos of contemporary Japanese suburbia, they are invariably welcomed by the neighborhood. Despite their aggressive appearance in photographs, in reality, they recede into the background. The interiors are equally immaculate; the inclusion of a large dedicated storeroom allows daily living areas to be kept empty of everything except the few items actively in use.

The FOB Homes system is partly an attempt to reunite modernist aesthetics (minimalist white boxes) with modernist ideology (democratic, affordable design). FOB Homes thereby joins a lineage comprising far more failure than success, whether due to co-option by a wealthy elite, as in the California Case Study Houses, or outright rejection by the intended inhabitants, as in Le Corbusier's Pessac housing estate. Perhaps only in Japan, where simplicity has always signified luxury, are such ambitions plausible.

FOB Homes Typologies /

Type A: Outside/Inside

With mostly blank exterior walls, this prototype is intended for a lot in a typical housing subdivision.

    The internal courtyard and the double-height main hall form a single, continuous space. The exterior is brought into the hall, and the interior extended to the courtyard. The various domestic activities are distributed without clear room divisions.

Type B: Common/Private + Figure/Ground

This prototype is based on the relationship of shared and private zones being reversed between the upper level and the lower level.

    On the lower level, the living area is surrounded by a number of closed "servant spaces." On the upper level, private sleeping areas are separated by open "light voids." The latter contain windows oriented perpendicular to the exterior walls, bringing in light while maintaining privacy.

Type C: Single Space Made Visible

This prototype is intended for a long and narrow site, the "eel's nest."

    Functional zones are defined by a row of glazed courtyards, which are used to bring in light and air, along the main tubular volume. The two longitudinal walls incorporate full-height storage units. The basic house may act as the foundation for an upper level.

Type D: Transparent/Opaque

With all external openings concentrated on one face, this prototype is intended for larger residential developments.

    The site is divided into parallel zones that range from opaque to transparent. This spatial sequence defines the functional layout: from storage areas to private rooms to shared living spaces to the adjacent garden.

Type E: Flexibility from Storage Space

This prototype is intended for relatively open sites. Natural ventilation is optimized by concentrating the majority of openings on two opposite walls.

    The "servant space" is located centrally; the internal wall surfaces are covered entirely with shelving. On the upper level, a shared activity space can contain personal possessions that overflow from the adjacent sleeping areas; this minimizes the necessary floor area for the sleeping quarters and thus maximizes the size of the shared space.

173

	hall
	kitchen
	bathroom
	storage
	utility
	bedroom
	entrance
	garden
	terrace

Possible expansion of the basic typologies

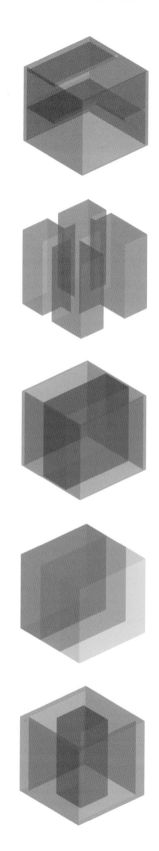

A

B

C

D

E

Possible spatial variations of the basic typologies

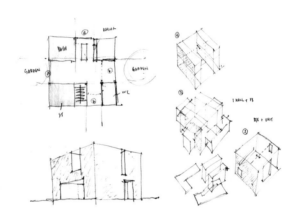

Prototypes in Suburbia /

Peter Allison

With the multiple-choice house catalogs of Japan's "housemaker" companies in mind, FOBA have developed a range of prototype designs known as FOB Homes, that are intended to address the various site conditions encountered in Japanese suburbia. The inspiration for this approach came from a specific FOBA project: the F-House, located in the suburbs of Osaka and completed in 2000. While responding to the particular needs of its client, this design included a range of innovations within a spatial concept that, as it happens, is the antithesis of the organizational characteristics of the typical housemaker plan. Compared to the exterior, a white rectangular solid with a few discrete openings, the interior layout of the F-House is remarkably fluid. Related functions are not always situated next to one another, as convention would suggest; a short journey—down a passage, up stairs, or across a bridge—is required to get from one space to another. As a result of this separation, it is possible to create a sense of seclusion and privacy, where appropriate, while avoiding the compartmentalization that results from the use of doors. Spaces contract and expand rhythmically, producing an architectural landscape in which activities gravitate naturally to their own unique location.

The strategic purpose of the external wall is to claim the maximum volume of space for the use of the occupants. Rather than a small peripheral garden, two large open spaces—one internal and one external—are situated at the heart of the F-House plan. According to the architects, these are the shared

177

Typical "housemaker" houses in contemporary Japanese suburbia spaces that support daily life in the house. On either side, private spaces are arranged in two narrow bands, yet due to their connection with the common spaces, they do not seem cramped. The interior can be seen as a single space whose indented volume is contained within a single continuous wall. Where it follows the site boundary, this wall remains mostly unbroken, whereas within the site, it is perforated by large structural openings. Whether fitted with fixed or operable glazing, or simply left open to frame internal and external views, the dramatic changes in the sectional profile of this element contribute sub-stantially to the spatial dynamics of the house.

The F-House was extended into a series of prototypes by dismantling the original design into a series of architectural components. The identity of the shared space, for instance, was developed based on the relationship between its internal and external components, and on the stepped section formed by the terrace on the second floor. By adjusting to the sizes and geometries of alternative sites, the prototypes became appropriate variations on the basic arrangement. Further inventions that the F-House made available for reuse in other circumstances include the design of the entrance as a deep recess in a blank wall, the provision of a generous amount of storage space in a highly accessible location, the design of the staircase as a light-framed structure that does not interfere with the possibility of creating long sightlines within the house, and a language of external openings with translucent glazing at ground level for privacy and larger openings on the second floor, where attaining privacy is less of a problem.

FOB Homes marketing brochures

The abstract sites for which the prototypes were designed have different proportional relationships between street frontage and site depth, and the prototypes anticipate being surrounded by other houses of a similar scale. Prototypes A and B were both conceived for typical subdivision lots, with Type A following the F-House model. Type B follows the same principles in developing a reversal in the pattern of solid and void between its two main floors. Type C uses small courtyards as a way to create deep sites with narrow frontages, known as "eel's nest" sites. Types D and E are intended for sites with wider frontages and less depth. In Type D, all the openings face in the same direction; Type E contains an exceptionally large storeroom in a central position. In order to provide a more direct alternative to the typical commissioning process, information about FOB Homes is freely available through FOB Co-op, a chain of stores selling household goods and fashion items, based in Tokyo and with branches throughout the country.[1]

As an approach to the design of nonluxury housing, the FOB Homes prototypes have two great strengths: they identify a set of principles and demonstrate their relevance in a range of situations while remaining open to further development in discussion with individual clients. In this respect, the FOB Homes system shares certain methodological principles with Le Corbusier's residential projects of the 1920s. In addition to the Five Points for a New Architecture (the free-standing column, the roof garden, the free plan, the ribbon window, and the free facade), Le Corbusier proposed a series of distinctive built volumes that were intended to address the conditions on different types of

1 / FOB Co-op was founded in 1981 by Mitsue Masunaga, a Japanese businesswoman, to bring European-made products to Japan. Katsu Umebayashi is Masunaga's nephew.

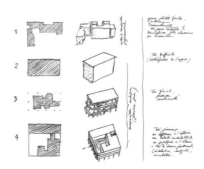

Le Corbusier, *Les quatre compositions*

sites.[2] He illustrated these volumes with sketches of his own designs: the L-shaped block of the La Roche-Jeanneret double house (1923), the closed rectangular form of the Villa Stein de Monzie (1927), the rectangular but permeable form of the Villa Baizea in Carthage (1929), and the horizontal slab of the Villa Savoye (1930).[3] The enormous versatility of his approach derived from the loose fit between the architectural components, described in the Five Points, and the volumetric profile of the project in which they were expected to play a significant role. A similar flexibility is displayed by the FOB Homes system: variations on the prototypes develop a momentum of their own and reveal possibilities that the prototypes themselves did not envisage.

The most controversial aspect of FOB Homes concerns the relationship between the houses and their immediate context. FOB Homes are almost inevitably surrounded by generic housemaker homes. With predictably narrow strips of planting around the edges of each plot and with windows looking directly at their neighbors, these homes are relentlessly similar in character. As illustrated in the housemaker marketing brochures, one way of establishing identity in this environment is to have a European car parked in front. The exteriors of FOB Homes are ambiguous in scale: they can be seen as two-story structures or large-scale single-story structures, depending on one's point of view. In this respect, they are not dissimilar to the *machiya* (the traditional townhouse, examples of which still survive in places such as Kyoto's Gion district), in the masklike countenance they present toward the street—suggestive yet discreet. Instead of the outward

2 / Peter Behrens et al., *Bau und Wohnung: Die Bauten der Weissenhof-Siedlungen in Stuttgart* (Stuttgart: Deutscher Werkbund, 1927), 27.

3 / Le Corbusier and Pierre Jeanneret, *Oeuvre Complète, Vol. 1 1910–29* (Zurich: Girsberger, 1936), 189.

Typical *machiya* in the Gion district of Kyoto

glare of the housemaker designs, FOB Homes are visually self contained, and the only hint of their internal organization comes from the setbacks on the upper floors.

In many ways, their appearance inverts the attributes of the housemaker homes, but, being similar in size, they respect the spirit—if not the letter—of continuity. As well as enhancing the privacy of their neighbors, their appearance punctuates and questions the expansive picture of which they are a very small part. The urban design potential of FOB Homes can only become clearer as more multiple-unit projects are completed.

In parallel with promoting an alternative view of the role of housing in city formation, the FOB Homes system is also an investigation of the vexed question of the relationship between spatial imagery and patterns of occupation. In social housing, the long-term commitment to building units of a restricted size on a repetitive basis has been ultimately counterproductive due to the difficulty of accommodating future changes and expectations within this framework.

On this basis, Le Corbusier's housing at Pessac might be considered a success: with relatively generous floor areas and a certain organizational boldness, it has been able to accommodate patterns of occupation quite different from those envisaged by the architect.[4] In his classic houses of the 1920s, the scale of the main reception space, conceived as a studio-type environment for the display of furniture and works of art, plays a dominant role in the internal organization and the external appearance of each project. There is the clear outline of a similar

4 / As described by Philippe Boudon in *Lived-in Architecture: Le Corbusier's Pessac Revisited* (London: Lund Humphries, 1972).

atelier-type space at the heart of the F-House,
along with a possible reference to Case Study House
#25 (1962) in Long Beach, California, designed by
Killingsworth, Brady, & Smith. As a development of
the U-shaped plan typology explored in other Case
Study houses, the main spaces in the Killingsworth
house address the long side of a two-story-high
enclosed court. With sliding glass doors to the living
and dining areas, an easy exchange between inside
and outside was intended, but the use of these spaces
has been restricted by a somewhat narrow view of
how they should be furnished.

　　In the F-House, the relationship between the
internal and external shared spaces is reminiscent of
that between an auditorium and stage—except it
is not clear which is which. When the glazed doors
separating the two spaces are slid aside, the
horizontal opening forms a proscenium arch visible
from inside or out, and the upper-level private
space and terrace function as theater boxes over-
looking the area below. This effect is particularly clear
in photographs that show the house with a bare
minimum of furnishings—not necessarily a misleading
effect, given the generous proportions of the nearby
storeroom.

　　Both the interior and exterior of the houses
are painted white in order to provide a neutral back-
drop that will support a wide range of activities.
Unlike the Case Study houses, neither the furniture
nor its layout are permanent fixtures because they
can be cleared away and replaced by other items from
the storeroom. In many respects, this arrangement
reinterprets the tradition of temporary displays, known
as kazari, which informed traditional craft production

in Japan and is still practiced today.[5] Historically, this involved the use of moveable furniture, such as folding screens, scroll paintings, ceramics, lacquerware, and flower displays, which were intended to transform the identity of a space so that it provided a more sympathetic environment for a particular event or activity. When not required, they were kept in purpose-built storage. In the F-House, the same principle provides a coherent basis for the periodic use of the aesthetically incongruous products that are a normal part of the contemporary domestic environment.[6]

As the immediate precedent for a wider system, the F-House will remain a special case. Its worth as a model can only be assessed by evaluating the relevance of the principles it demonstrates to the various situations in which they have been applied. Both the T-House and the I-House occupy very restricted sites and include a single parking space, a requirement that was not part of the F-House brief. To be as open as possible, the shared space is situated at the upper floor level in the T-House, while in the I-House, it is situated at ground level and extends into the parking court when the car is absent. The I-House is especially dense, with four private spaces, whereas the shared spaces in the K-House are similar in scale to those of the F-House due to the more spacious sites the latter two occupy. The H-House uses a part of its external space for parking and has storage rooms on both floors.

The litmus test of any systematized approach to residential design is whether or not it succeeds in producing houses that are supportive and responsive to the needs and aspirations of their occupants; which

5 / As noted in the exhibition Kazari: Decoration and Display in Japan, 15th–19th Centuries at the British Museum, London, 2003, *kazari* (literally "decoration") is the world of dynamic display in premodern Japan. It refers both to the decoration of individual objects and to their combination in displays for special occasions. It was used in many contexts: the shogun's special "guest hall," the brothels of the Yoshiwara pleasure quarter, and the great annual festivals in Japanese cities.

6 / For photographic documentation of Japanese residential interiors without built-in storage, see Kyoichi Tsuzuki's *Tokyo Style* (Tokyo: Chikuma Shobo, 1993) and *Tokyo: A Certain Style* (San Francisco: Chronicle Books, 1999).

183

is to say, whether or not the system is capable of producing a domestic environment. In this respect, FOB Homes is a resounding success. In *The Poetics of Space*, Gaston Bachelard uses references from literary history to make a powerful case for the design of houses where the main elements provide an immediately recognizable series of distinctive experiences: each floor should have a different character, the quality of light should vary from one space to another space, the exterior should have a definite presence in relation to its surroundings, and so on.[7] Looking at the built examples of FOB Homes, it is clear that these criteria have been met.

7 / Gaston Bachelard, *The Poetics of Space*, trans. Maria Jolas (Boston: Beacon Press, 1969).

F-House /

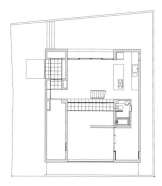

Plans, scale 1:400

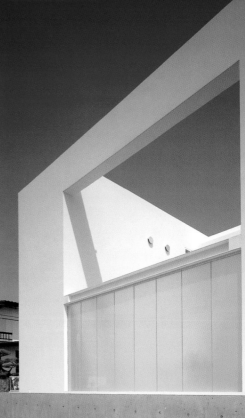

H-House /

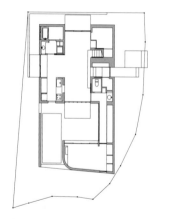 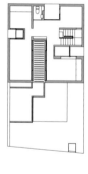

Plans, scale 1:400

T-House/

Plans, scale 1:400

K-House /

Plans, scale 1:400

I-House /

Plans, scale 1:400

F-Blanc /

Plans of two basic apartment types:

Maisonette type A (left) and B (right), scale 1:400

Afterword /

Kazuhiro Kojima

Katsu Umebayashi is, I would say, the odd one out among the new generation of young Japanese architects. You just need to meet him once to be overwhelmed by his unbridled energy. He's what we call *yancha*. That's an expression from the dialect of the Kansai area, where both Katsu and I were born. *Yancha* means "lovable rogue," which pretty much sums up his character.

 I sometimes feel that I'm everywhere at once, but Katsu seems truly omnipresent. In 2003, a project of mine called Space Blocks was completed in Hanoi, Vietnam. I half jokingly sent out invitations to the opening ceremony, although I never believed that any of my busy colleagues would travel all that distance to attend. But Katsu actually showed up! In Hanoi, he talked like a machine-gun and drank like a fish, and,

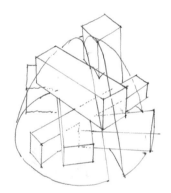  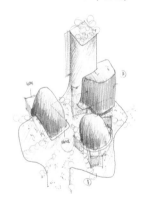

219

on top of that, he was able to fit in a few business meetings before he went home.

 He's always full of great stories—like the time he went to procure materials from some old workshop he had discovered deep in Eastern Europe or his many expeditions throughout Asia. You can hardly respond to these tales. You can only admire his vitality.

 Members of the younger generation of Japanese architects are generally known for their proficiency and confidence in the design of small houses. His *yancha* personality aside, Katsu has also been producing sensitive and high-quality work. But don't be fooled. Rather than focusing his creative energy on individual projects, his priority is to create prototypical spaces with the power to be expanded, adapted, and replicated.

 In his attitude towards the design of architecture, Katsu has a certain affinity with his peer Yoshiharu Tsukamoto of Atelier Bow-Wow. Yet while Tsukamoto continues developing a theoretical approach that he presents in books such as *Made in Tokyo*, Katsu is far more interested in actual, physical objects.

It is not insignificant that Katsu is based in Kyoto, the area of Japan where the weight of history is heaviest. I am not sure if I should mention this, but he hails from a family of long-established Japanese tea manufacturers. From a Western point of view, this may seem like a typical Japanese heritage. In fact, Japanese people with such a background are quite rare (we are not all sumo wrestlers or samurai). Does this background affect the space and architecture he creates? Yes, I believe it does. His *yancha* character—bold enough to be intimidated by nothing, yet somehow winsome—is reinforced by his unique background. Katsu has a natural comprehension of Japanese history. With culture behind him, Katsu is able to confront and engage it all: modernism, the traditional townhouses of Kyoto, sometimes even postmodernism.

I hope he continues to attempt the unprecedented. Even though I know him very well, I can never predict what he'll do next. I've always had great expectations, and still do. I'll have to keep my eye on him—both as a rival and as a friend.

Selected Bibliography /

Books /

10 City Profiles. Tokyo: Toto Shuppan, 2001, 96–135.

Daniell, Thomas. "Case Study 1." In *Japan Concrete*, edited by Mil De Kooning et al., cover, 119–47. Ghent: A&S Books, 2004.

———. "Containment." In *Portable Architecture and Unpredictable Surroundings*, edited by Pilar Echavarría, 144–47. Barcelona: Structure, 2005.

Flagge, Ingeborg, ed. *Jahrbuch Licht und Architektur*. Cologne: Rudolf Müller GmbH, 2000, 184–89.

———. *Postmodernism Revisited*. Hamburg: Junius Verlag, 2004, 188–89.

Gaventa, Sarah. *Concrete Design*. London: Mitchell Beazley, 2001, 114–15.

Kira, Moriko and Mariko Terada, eds. *Towards Totalscape*. Rotterdam: NAi Publishers, 2000, 72, 128–29.

La Biennale di Venezia Expo Online: Less Aesthetics More Ethics. Barcelona: Actar, 2000, 114–17, CD-rom.

Mostaedi, Arian, ed. *Sustainable Architecture: High-tech Housing*. California: Gingko Press, 2003, 46–56.

Nosé, Michiko Rico and Michael Freeman. *Design Japan*. London: Mitchell Beazley, 2004, 84–85, 104–7.

Pople, Nicolas. *Experimental Houses*. London: Laurence King Publishing, 2000, 28–33.

Rössler, Hannes, ed. *Minihäuser in Japan*. Salzburg: Verlag Anton Pustet, 2000, 17–25.

Schittich, Christian, ed. *In Detail: Japan*. Munich: Detail/Birkhäuser, 2002, 86–89.

Serrats, Marta, ed. *Capturing Space*. New York: Harper Collins, 2004, 46–53.

Soane, James. *New Home*. London: Conran Octopus, 2003, cover, 51, 176–79.

Stiller, Adolph, ed. *45 under 45: Young Architecture Japan*. Salzburg: Verlag Anton Pustet, 2002, 38–39.

Umebayashi, Katsu et al. "Designers' House Builders." In *AB Design*, edited by Yasuo Kondo, B203–B222. Tokyo: Rikuyosha, 2003.

———. *FOB Homes*. Tokyo: Inax Shuppan, 2005.

Periodicals /

Arieff, Alison. "Osaka: A Slice of Life." *Dwell* 2, no. 5 (June 2002): 38–40.

"Aura." *Arch+* 151 (July 2000): 42–45.

"Aura." *Kenchiku Bunka* 51, no. 595 (May 1996): 72–80.

Barrie, Andrew. "10 x 10." *Monument* 41 (April/May 2001): 54–65.

Bullivant, Lucy. "Japan: Down, But Not Out." *World Architecture*, June 2001, 42–45.

"Casas Aura y Strata." *ViA Arquitectura*, no. 7 (January 2000): 122–27.

Daniell, Thomas. "Architects as 'Housemakers' in Japan." *Architectural Design*, July 2003, 82–89.

———. "Fitting in: Small Sites in Urban Japan." *L'Architecture d'Aujourd'hui* 328 (June 2000): 80–84.

———. "FOB Homes." *Arch+* 158 (September 2001): 100–103.

———. "Manufacturing a Market." *L'Architecture d'Aujourd'hui* 338 (January 2002): 102–5.

———. "Stripped-Down Expressionism." *Archis*, December 1996, 11–12.

"FOBA." *Lotus* 111 (2001): 18–21.

Fox, Dan. "Fuksas' Good Fight." *World Architecture*, June 2000, 34–35.

Geudens, Helga. "Logement de Série pas comme les Autres." *Decors* 1014 (March 2002): 241–45.

———. "Le Concept de la Maison Vide." *Decors* 1013 (December 2001): 75–79.

———. "Organismes Architectoniques." *Decors* 1015 (June 2002): 144–47.

———. "Un Origami Géant." *Decors* 1015 (June 2002): 148–51.

Hönig, Roderick. "Fertighaus nach Mass." *NZZ Folio*, no. 7 (July 2002): 54–55.

"House in Mineyama." *Detail*, November 2002, 1406–9.

"House in Uozaki." *GA Japan* 25, 3–4 (1997): 152–53.

"Ichiban." *Wired*, September 2001, 120–25.

Kinoshita, Toshiko. "Pret-a-Porter Houses." *JT* 180 (April 2001): 48–63.

Klauser, Wilhelm. "Zwerghausen, Vorgefertigt." *Archithese*, March/April 2003, 60–65.

"Light Cage (Y House)." *GA Japan* 31, 3–4 (1998): 120–21.

Ohno, Shigekazu. "Natural x Modern Houses." *Esquire*, Japan edition, December 2003, 126–47.

"Orient, Aura, Stack." *Zlaty Rez* 21 (Winter 2000): cover, 52–59.

Pollock, Naomi. "This House is a Product." *Dwell* 1, no. 5 (June 2001): 70–77.

"Single Family House in Tokyo." *Detail*, September 2000, 1009–11.

"Strata." *JT* 148 (August 1998): 154–59.

"Tent for Urban Nomads." *L'Architecture d'Aujourd'hui* 320 (January 1999): 102–5.

"Thin Skin." *Architektur & Bauforum*, no. 204 (Jan/Feb 2000): 50–51.

Umebayashi, Katsu. "Kyoto Model." *JT* 206 (June 2003): 114–23.

———. "Organ." *JA* 23 (Autumn 1996): 96–103.

———. "Pleats." *JA* 39 (Autumn 2000): 114–23.

———. "Pleats." *JT* 177 (January 2001): 58–73.

Van Sande, Hera. "Mountain of Steps." *Archis*, October 2003, 104–9.

Webb, Michael. "Stepped Box." *Architectural Review*, May 2004, 86–89.

Wilson, Christopher. "The New Japanese House: A Question of Emphasis." *Cross Section*, April 2003, 12–13.

Wöhler, Anke. "Elegant Falten(t)wurf." *DBZ*, April 2002, 72–75.

———. "Zurückgezogene Schönheit." *DBZ*, October 2001, cover, 68–71.

"Wohnhaus in Tokio." *Deutsche Bauzeitung*, January 1997, cover, 70–73.

Author Biographies /

Katsu Umebayashi is an architect and the founder and director of FOBA.

Thomas Daniell is an architect and was a member of FOBA from 1995 to 2005.

Michael Webb is an architecture critic based in Los Angeles.

Peter Allison is a writer and curator based in London.

Kazuhiro Kojima is an architect and is the founding partner of C+A, Tokyo.

Image Credits /

© 2004 Artists Rights Society (ARS), New York/ADAGP, Paris/FLC: 179
Corbis: 40, 118, 158
Thomas Daniell: Back cover, 8–15, 24–26, 36, 42, 58, 60, 72, 74, 86, 99, 104, 120, 136, 144, 146, 177, 180, 216–17
Akihiko Endo: Endsheets
Hiroyuki Hirai: Cover BL and BR, 64–67, 70, 88, 92–97, 102
Atelier Iijima: 212–15
Junichi Kato: 106
Toshiyuki Kobayashi: 110–13, 116, 168, 186–91, 200–211
Kazushi Nakauji/agnès b. Sunrise Inc.: 152–53
Yasumori Shimoura: 193–95
Shinkenchiku-sha: Cover TL, 46–51, 56, 124, 126R, 127, 196–99
Kazuumi Takahashi: 150–51, 156
Courtesy of Tokugawa Gallery: 134
Osamu Tsuda: 78–81, 84, 125, 126L, 132, 138–39, 142
Tohru Waki/Shokokusha: Cover TR, 28, 32–35, 38

Sketches: Katsu Umebayashi
Computer graphics: Akihiko Endo

Text Credits /

Project texts: Thomas Daniell
Translation from Japanese (Kazuhiro Kojima's essay): Sawako Akune
Translation from Japanese (Katsu Umebayashi's essay): Thomas Daniell